Contents

Alfred Music
P.O. Box 10003
Van Nuys, CA 91410-0003
alfred.com

Book
ISBN-10: 0-7390-8615-4   ISBN-13: 978-0-7390-8615-5
Book and CD
ISBN-10: 0-7390-8616-2   ISBN-13: 978-0-7390-8616-2
CD
ISBN-10: 0-7390-8617-0   ISBN-13: 978-0-7390-8617-9

Front cover photos: Banjo courtesy of Gibson USA • Photo of Janet Robin by Kevin Estrada
Back cover photo models: Sheyna Gee (top), Facebook.com/sheynageemusic • Mark Burgess
(middle left) • Dick Weissman (bottom)
Back cover photos: Top: Greg Pidfigurny • Middle left: Larry Lytle

CD recorded by Dick Weissman.

 Alfred Cares. Contents printed on environmentally responsible paper.

The Parts of Your Banjo

The following are the parts that make up a banjo. Note that banjos can come with or without resonators, and arm rests may not be found on all banjos.

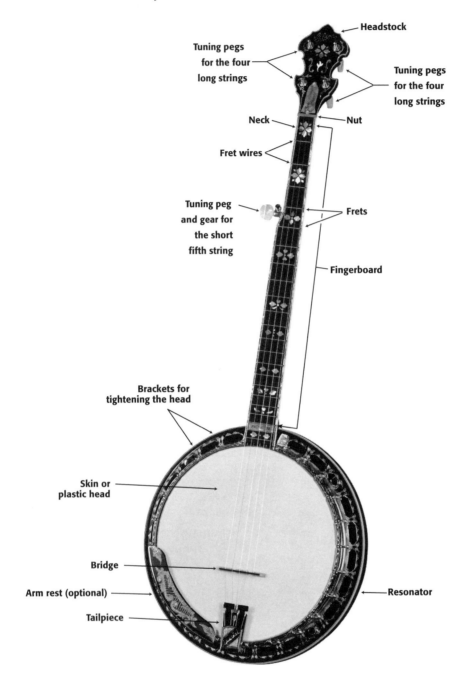

Choosing a Banjo

If you have a teacher, ask them for recommendations when looking for a banjo. Banjo makers range from Goldtone and Deering, who produce reasonably priced banjos that are ideal for beginners, to OME and Gibson, who make the higher-priced models. If you choose to buy a used banjo, look for ease of playing (with the height of strings above neck, not difficult to push down) and quality of tone. When shopping for a used banjo, bring a teacher or friend who already plays to inspect the instrument. Most importantly, do not buy a banjo with a warped neck!

How to Hold Your Banjo

Sitting or Standing

The best way to begin practicing or playing your banjo is in a seated position. You can either play with both feet flat on the floor or with your legs crossed. Be careful, though, since crossing your legs for prolonged periods may be uncomfortable.

While seated, you may need a strap. However, a strap is always needed when playing in a standing position. If you wear the banjo too low while standing, you will find reaching for the strings uncomfortable. Be sure to use a sturdy strap because the weight of the instrument is largely in the head, and you want to be sure that the banjo feels stable while you are playing.

Seated with feet flat on floor.

Seated with legs crossed.

Standing with strap.

Seated with strap.

Setting Up Your Banjo

Placing the Bridge

The first thing you should understand is that the banjo has a movable bridge. If a banjo is placed in a car trunk or shipped on an airplane, the bridge will move, and you will have to re-tune the instrument. The bridge is placed on the head of the banjo; the distance between the nut and the 12th fret must be exactly the same as the distance between the 12th fret and the spot on the banjo head where the bridge is placed. *Make sure the bridge is properly placed before attempting to tune the banjo.*

Tightening the Head

It is important for the head of a banjo to be tight so that the banjo produces the kind of crisp tone for which it is famous. Your banjo should come with a tool that resembles an old-fashioned skate key. This tuning key is used to tighten the brackets around the head. Go around the head and tighten every other bracket by a quarter turn. Then go around again and tighten the ones you missed. Flick your fingernail against the head. If you get a dull "thunk" sound, repeat the steps above until you get a bright snapping sound.

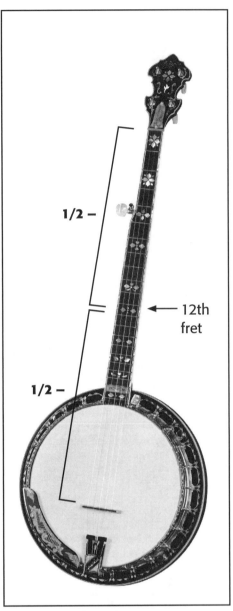

1/2 —

← 12th fret

1/2 —

The distance between the nut and the 12th fret should be equal to the distance between the 12th fret and the bridge.

Tuning key.

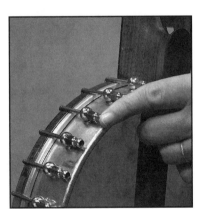

Close-up of brackets.

Checking to See That the Bridge Is Placed Properly

After the bridge is placed, play the 1st string open and then at the 12th fret; the two notes should be exactly one *octave* apart. An octave is the musical interval of eight notes, the higher of which has the same name as the lower but vibrates twice as fast.

If you have placed the bridge correctly but the banjo still isn't in tune, it's possible that the banjo neck is warped or set up at the wrong angle. If this is the case, have the instrument checked out at a musical instrument repair shop. Sometimes it's difficult to tune the banjo because the screws that hold the gears in the tuning pegs have become loose. You can tighten them by using a very small, thin screwdriver.

See page 63 for additional information on banjo heads, strings, bridges, and fingerpicks.

How to Tune Your Banjo

Tuning to a Keyboard

The five strings of the banjo are the same pitches as the five notes shown here on the piano:

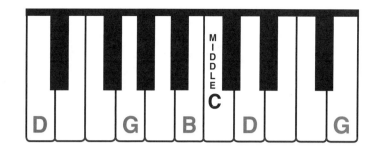

Tuning with the CD
Track 1

Included on the audio recording are complete tuning instructions. Before tuning, make sure the bridge is in the right place.

Tuning to a Guitar

You can tune your banjo to a guitar by matching the following notes:

- Open 1st string of the banjo to 2nd string, 3rd fret of the guitar
- Open 2nd, 3rd, and 4th strings of the banjo to open 2nd, 3rd, and 4th strings of the guitar
- Open 5th string of the banjo to 1st string, 3rd fret of the guitar

Tuning the Banjo to Itself
Track 2

The following method shows how to tune the banjo when you don't have a tuner, piano, or guitar to tune to.

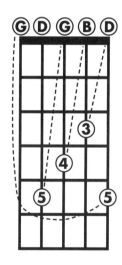

1. Tighten the 1st string until it sounds clear and does not rattle against the frets when played open
2. Match the sound of the 2nd string, 3rd fret with that of the 1st string open
3. Match the sound of the 3rd string, 4th fret to that of the 2nd string open
4. Match the sound of the 4th string, 5th fret with that of the 3rd string open
5. Match the sound of the 5th string open with that of the 1st string played at the 5th fret

The diagram to the right illustrates this method.

Electronic Tuners

Even with all these options to tune your banjo, the first accessory you should purchase is an electronic tuner. They cost anywhere from $10–$30 and up, depending on how many features you think you may need. You can also purchase an inexpensive tuning app for your smartphone or other device.

To use the tuner, play a string and the needle (or lights) of the tuner will move left and right. If you are tuned too high (*sharp*), the tuner will move across the center line to the right; if you are tuned too low (*flat*), it will be left of center. Make sure to buy a *chromatic* tuner (one that has all of the notes, including sharps and flats). That way, you can tune while using a capo (we'll discuss more about capos later). You can also tune a guitar, mandolin, or any other instrument that you might play with a chromatic tuner.

The Left Hand

The left-hand fingers are numbered as follows:

Index = 1

Middle = 2

Ring = 3

Pinky = 4

Thumb = T

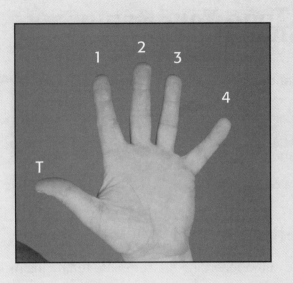

Placing the Left-Hand Fingers

Track 3

In order to get a clear sound from the banjo, the left-hand fingers must press firmly on the strings directly behind (not on!) the frets. See the photos below for correct and incorrect finger placement.

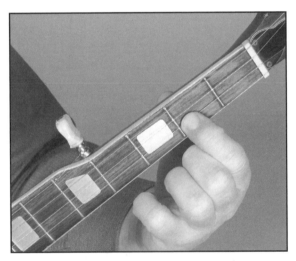

Correct! Finger presses the string down near the fret without actually being on it.

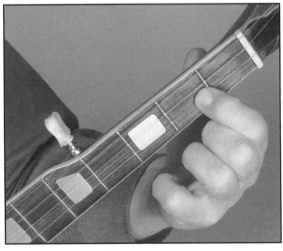

Wrong! Finger is too far from the fret wire; tone is "buzzy" and indefinite.

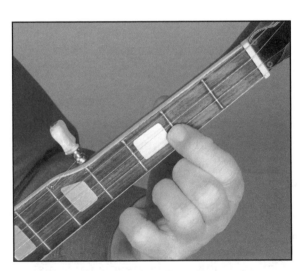

Wrong! Finger is on top of the fret wire; tone is muffled and unclear.

The Right Hand

The right-hand fingers are lettered like this:

Index = I

Middle = M

Ring = R

Pinky (not used)

Thumb = T

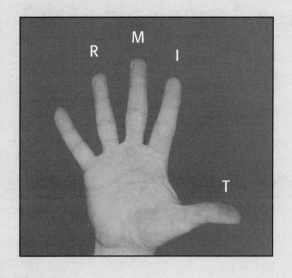

Picking with the Right Hand

The right hand is used to pick the notes. When picks are used, the following is almost always true: 1. The thumb picks away from the body, 2. The fingers pick toward the body. This is especially true when seated but is often the case when standing.

Any right-hand fingering combination is called a *strum*. A strum can be as simple as one movement across the strings with the fingers or as complicated as an advanced combination of thumb strokes and finger strokes used in bluegrass.

Picks

Although the five-string banjo can be played with bare fingers, many players, especially those interested in bluegrass, prefer using a plastic thumb pick and metal finger picks on the index and middle fingers of the right hand.

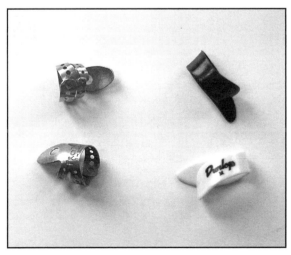

Various plastic and metal picks.

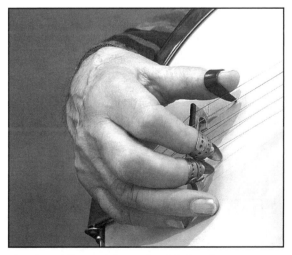

Thumb and finger picks on the right hand.

Getting Acquainted with Tablature

The Staff

Banjo music is most often notated in a system called *tablature* (or TAB). Tablature is handy because, unlike standard music notation, it relates specifically to the instrument for which it's written. In banjo TAB, each line of a five-line staff represents one of the banjo's strings. The bottom line represents the 5th (short) string, the next line up represents the 4th string, the line up from that the 3rd string, and so on.

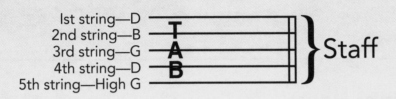

Numbering the Notes

A "0" on the first (top) line, for example, indicates that you should play the 1st string open (not fretted). A "2" on the 3rd line indicates to place one of your left-hand fingers on the 3rd string at the 2nd fret.

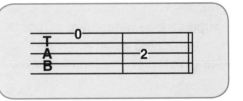

Right-hand indications are found beneath the staff. A "T" means to play with the thumb, an "I" with the index finger and an "M" with the middle finger. This example tells you to strum (play with a quick sweeping motion) all the open strings with the thumb.

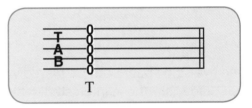

Measures, Bar Lines, and Beats

Music is divided into *measures,* or bars, marked off by vertical lines called *bar lines*. In most tunes, measures represent equal units of musical time. Measures, in turn, are divided into equal units of time called *beats.* Think of the beats in a measure in terms of your own heartbeat—a steady, even, recurring pulse.

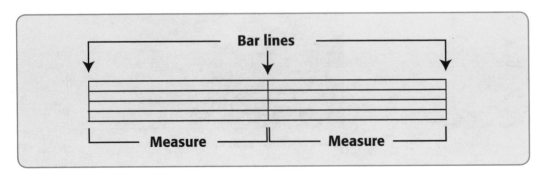

Sound-Off: How to Count Time

Quarter Notes and Eighth Notes

In most banjo music, the *value* (that is, the duration) of a single beat is expressed as a *quarter note.* All other notes are expressed in relation to this value and may be thought of in terms of fractions. A note half as long as a quarter note is therefore called an *eighth note;* two eighth notes equal one quarter note. In TAB, quarter notes are notated with a vertical line called a *stem* that descends from the number on the staff; single eighth notes add a flag to the stem, while eighth notes in groups are joined by a heavy line called a *beam.*

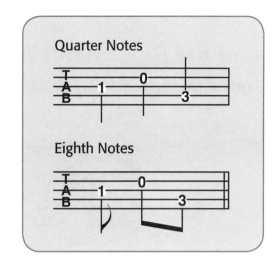

Quarter Notes

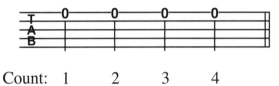

Count: 1   2   3   4

Eighth Notes

Count: 1 & 2 & 3 & 4 &

Time Signatures

Each piece of music has numbers at the beginning called a *time signature.* These numbers tell us how to count time. The TOP NUMBER tells us how many counts are in each measure. The BOTTOM NUMBER tells us what kind of note gets one count.

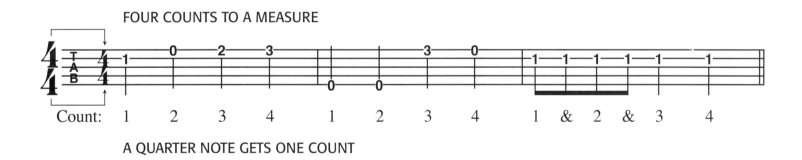

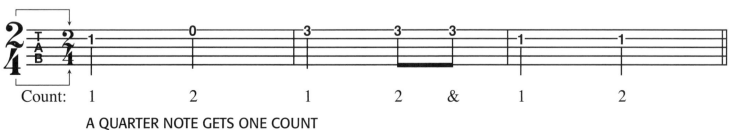

Right-Hand Picking

Position of the Right Hand When Playing

Rest your right-hand ring finger, and/or pinky, on the head of the banjo when playing.
See the photo below.

Different Ways to Pick the Strings with the Right Hand

In bluegrass music, it's customary to pick the strings close to the bridge. This results in a brighter sound.

For a different sound, try moving your hand down toward the neck, near the fingerboard. If you play right on the top of the neck, you will get a mellow sound—appropriate for old-time music, but not powerful enough to cut though when playing in a full bluegrass band.

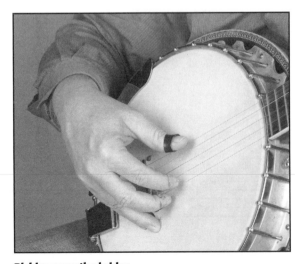

Picking near the bridge.

Picking near the fingerboard.

Use the thumb pick to play any note, except the 1st string. Pick away from the body with the thumb pick. The 1st string is played with the index finger, picking toward your body.

OPEN-STRING EXERCISE Track 4.1

Play the following open-string exercise (remember you are not using any left-hand fingers) while keeping a steady beat. Try counting "1 & 2 & 3 & 4 &" while playing. In this exercise, you are alternating your thumb and index finger: thumb, index, thumb, index, etc.

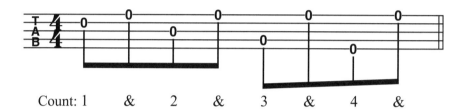

Count: 1 & 2 & 3 & 4 &

As you are playing, look down at your right hand to make sure the notes you are using are the ones notated. Once you are used to playing this sequence of notes, try to play them without looking at the banjo. This may seem impossible at first, but it really isn't that difficult. Soon, it will become natural to you.

Once you have mastered this right-hand technique, work on skipping strings by playing the strings as shown below. Once again, the thumb can play any string except the 1st string, and the index finger plays only the 1st string.

OPEN-STRING SEQUENCE Track 4.2

Now, let's try playing the following open-string sequence: 3 1 5 1, 2 1 4 1

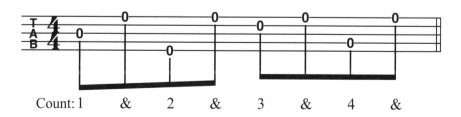

Count: 1 & 2 & 3 & 4 &

Practice this over and over until it becomes natural to you.

The D7 Chord

Track 5

Let's begin with the D7 chord.

Take a look at the diagram to the right. The dots indicate where to place your fingers. There are two dots in the diagram for the D7 chord, one on the 3rd string, and the other on the 2nd string. The dot on the 3rd string is at the 2nd fret, and the dot on the 2nd string is at the 1st fret. Under the diagram are numbers that tell you which left-hand fingers to use. An "o" means the string is played open.

Now finger the D7 chord with your left hand. With your right thumb, slowly play all the strings, starting with the 4th (heaviest) string. Always place your left-hand fingers just behind the frets for the best sound.

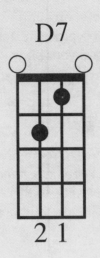

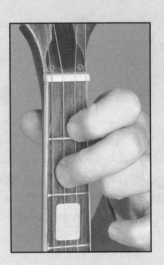

Note: In this book, all the chords will be indicated on four strings only. The 5th string (the short string that is closest to your body) won't be fingered here (although advanced players sometimes do finger it up the neck).

TROUBLESHOOTING

Be sure you are fingering directly behind the frets. If you're too close, or completely on the frets, you will get a muffled, buzzing sound. If you are getting a muffled sound with very little tone, there is a good chance you are not pressing hard enough with your left-hand fingers. Be sure to arch your wrist enough so that the 2nd finger on the 3rd string doesn't touch the 2nd string and interfere with its vibration. The photographs below give you examples of correct and incorrect fingerings.

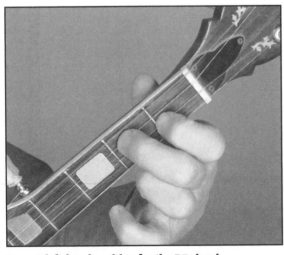

Correct left-hand position for the D7 chord.

Incorrect left-hand position for the D7 chord.

Changing Chords
Track 6

Now that you know the D7 chord, practice changing between the G chord (all open strings) and D7 chord. Start out by playing very slowly and evenly. When you see the symbol G followed by three slash marks **/ / /**, this means to use the right thumb to strum across the strings four times (once for the chord symbol and once each for the slash marks). Try the following exercise, and count while you play.

CHORD EXERCISE

G / / / | G / / / | G / / / | G / / / |
Count: 1 2 3 4   1 2 3 4   1 2 3 4   1 2 3 4

D7 / / / | D7 / / / | D7 / / / | D7 / / / |
1 2 3 4   1 2 3 4   1 2 3 4   1 2 3 4

G / / / | G / / / | G / / / | G / / / ‖
1 2 3 4   1 2 3 4   1 2 3 4   1 2 3 4

When you begin changing chords, look at your left hand to make sure that you are fingering the D7 chord correctly. Once you feel comfortable knowing where your left-hand fingers are going, play the exercise above without looking at your left hand.

MORE CHORD EXERCISES

Now try the same sequence but with more frequent chord changes.

Be sure to play slowly and evenly. Tap your foot each time you play a chord. If you can't change the chord without breaking the rhythm, slow down and gradually increase your speed as you get more comfortable changing chords.

G / / / | G / / / | D7 / / / | D7 / / / |
Count: 1 2 3 4   1 2 3 4   1 2 3 4   1 2 3 4

G / / / | D7 / / / | D7 / / / | G / / / ‖
1 2 3 4   1 2 3 4   1 2 3 4   1 2 3 4

Make up your own chord sequences as you become more confident with keeping the rhythm steady while changing chords. For example, try:

G / / / | D7 / / / | G / / / | D7 / / / | G / / / ‖
Count: 1 2 3 4   1 2 3 4   1 2 3 4   1 2 3 4   1 2 3 4

Once you master these chord changes, you will be ready to learn some new strums.

Half Note

In TAB, the position of a note in a measure is very important. A half note looks just like a quarter note, but in $\frac{2}{4}$, it is the only note in a measure. In $\frac{4}{4}$, it is half of a measure.

TRAIN ON THE ISLAND Track 7

"Train on the Island" is an old string-band tune. String bands play *roots* (old-time country) music and usually include banjo, guitar, fiddle, and mandolin. This song has no chord changes, so it will provide you with ample time to practice without having to worry about the left hand.

In this tune, there are two beats in each measure. The top line contains the melody in TAB notation, the lyrics, and the chord symbols (which, in this case, is only the G chord). The bottom line shows a sample strum with which you can accompany the melody. Just play the bottom part. Notice the thumb (T) and index finger (I) alternate throughout.

Ties

A *tie* is a curved line that connects two or more notes of the same pitch. When two notes are tied, the second one is not played; rather, the value is added to the first note.

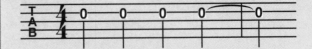

Hold the tied note two beats.

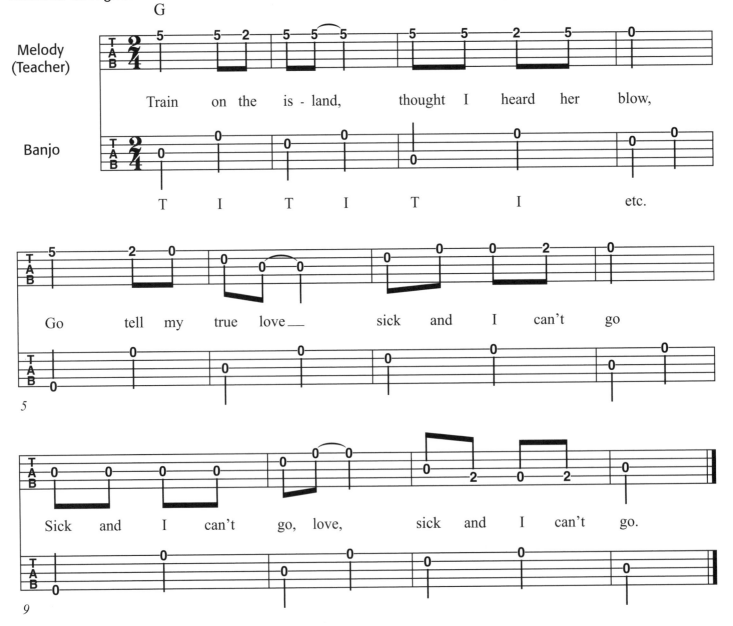

Introducing the Pinch

Track 8

When the thumb and index finger play at the same time, it is called a *pinch*. Let's learn a new strum sequence that uses the pinch. Here's a step-by-step breakdown of the strum sequence:

1. Thumb plays open 4th string

2. Thumb plays open 3rd string while index finger picks up on the open 1st string (together)

3. Thumb plays the open 5th string

4. Thumb plays the open 2nd string while the index finger picks up on the open 1st string

Here's what this strum looks like in TAB notation:

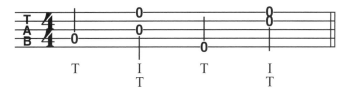

Since both the strums you have learned include four steps each, you can practice the same song with this strum. Listen to the recording to hear the strum alone and then with "Train on the Island." Then go back and play "Train on the Island" with the pinch strum.

Additional Lyrics for Train on the Island

Train on the island, headed for the west,
Goin' to see my true love, the one that I love best,
The one that I love best, love, the one that I love best.

Train on the island, thought I heard it squeal,
Go tell my true love, I can't roll the wheel,
I can't roll the wheel, love, I can't roll the wheel.

Train on the island, I thought I heard it squeal,
Go tell my true love, how happy I do feel,
How happy I do feel, love, how happy I do feel.

Train on the island, thought I heard it moan,
I'm living on an island, living all alone,
Living all alone, living all alone, love, living all alone.

Pinch Variations

Track 9

There are a number of other right-hand patterns that can be utilized with the pinch. Let's try adding the middle finger to the mix now. Here's another strum sequence:

1. Thumb plays open 4th string

2. Thumb plays open 3rd string while the middle finger plays the open 1st string (together)

3. Index finger plays the open 2nd string

4. Thumb plays the open 5th string

5. Middle finger plays the open 1st string

6. Thumb plays the open 3rd or 4th string

7. Index finger plays the open 2nd string

Note: The rhythm is now a quarter note followed by a series of eighth notes. That is, the first beat is twice as long as all the others. Try counting "1 2 & 3 & 4 &."

G

Count: 1   2 & 3 & 4 &   etc.

Once you can play the above fairly easily, pick whatever strings you'd like with the thumb in no particular order.

Below is the way the strum goes with the first four measures of "Train on the Island."

G

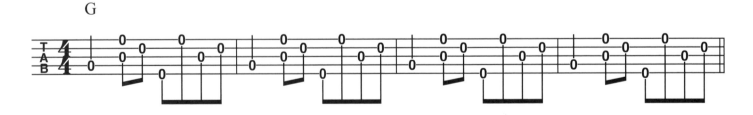

Try to figure out how the strum goes with the rest of "Train on the Island" on your own. If you get confused, listen to the recording and play along.

Three-Finger Pinch

Here is another pinch pattern that uses the thumb and two fingers to play together. As in the very first two-finger pattern that you learned on page 11, only the thumb moves around. The middle finger stays on the 1st string, and the index finger on the 2nd string. The pattern is:

1. Thumb plays the open 4th string or 5th string (alternate the notes each time you play)

2. The thumb plays the open 3rd string, while the index finger plays the open 2nd string and the middle finger plays the open 1st string (together)

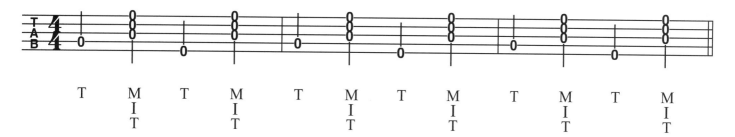

You should have no trouble fitting this strum into "Train on the Island."

For our final pinch variation, try this:

1. Thumb plays open 4th string

2. Thumb plays open 5th string, while the index finger plays the open 2nd string and the middle finger plays the open 1st string (together)

3. Thumb plays open 2nd string

4. Middle finger plays the open 1st string

5. Thumb plays the open 4th or 5th string

6. Index finger plays the open 3rd string

Track 10

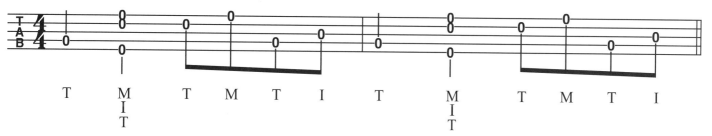

The rhythm here is two quarter notes followed by four eighth notes. Count "1 2 3 & 4 &" or long, long, short, short, short, short.

TROUBLESHOOTING

If your right-hand fingers are getting sore from wearing the picks, loosen them a bit, but not so much that they fall off your fingers or feel as though they will fall off. You can also bend the picks to suit the length and width of your fingers.

TOM DOOLEY Track 11

This song features your first chord change: G to D7 to G. An old North Carolina song based on a true incident, "Tom Dooley" was one of the key inspirations for the folk music revival of the late 1950s. It's a great song to learn, because it only has one simple chord change in measure 4. Included below are the melody, chords, and a simple strum. Play the bottom part.

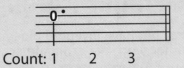

Dotted Half and Whole Notes

A *dotted half note* lasts three beats.

Count: 1   2   3

When you're in $\frac{4}{4}$ time and there is only one note in a measure with no stem, that note is a *whole note.* A whole note lasts four beats.

Count: 1   2   3   4

Moderately

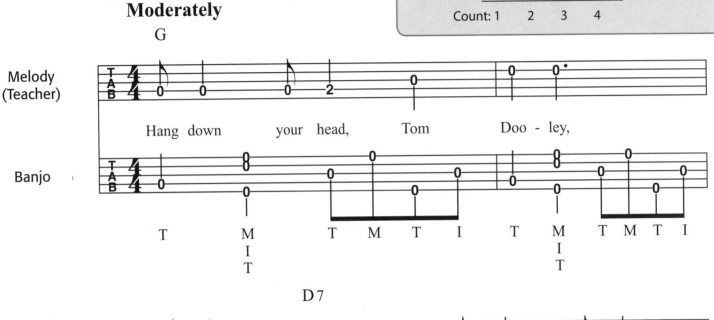

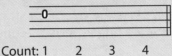

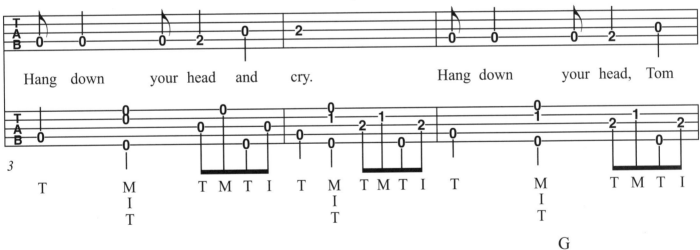

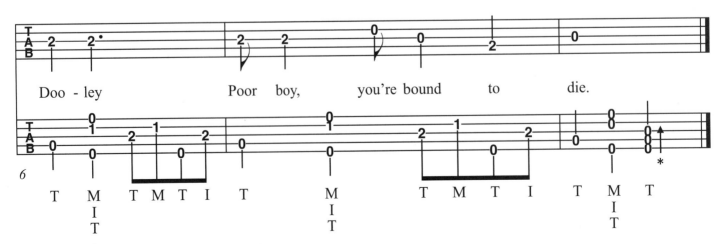

* This symbol (↑) means to strum down towards your body.

Earl Scruggs and the Roll

Earl Scruggs may not have invented bluegrass banjo, but he is probably more identified with it than any other banjo player. Scruggs learned to play in North Carolina from his older brother Junie and a wonderful banjo player named Snuffy Jenkins. Snuffy was one of the first players to perfect bluegrass banjo technique, and Scruggs formalized the right-hand picking pattern into sequences called *rolls.* A roll involves the use of the thumb, index, and middle fingers in patterns of eight eighth notes.

Scruggs became famous while playing with Bill Monroe, who is often called the "father of bluegrass." After leaving Monroe's band, Scruggs and legendary guitarist Lester Flatt played together for many years. Scruggs wrote many original banjo pieces, including "Foggy Mountain Breakdown," which was prominently featured in the movie *Bonnie and Clyde.*

The Forward Roll
Track 12

The *forward roll* is a roll in which the thumb (T), index (I), and middle (M) fingers pick the strings from the 5th string all the way to the 1st string. They move forward across the strings of the banjo, hence the name forward roll. Try the following:

1. Index finger picks upward on the 2nd string
2. Middle finger picks upward on the 1st string
3. Thumb picks downward on the 5th string
4. Index finger picks upward on the 2nd string
5. Middle finger picks upward on the 1st string
6. Thumb picks downward on the 5th string
7. Index finger picks upward on the 2nd string
8. Middle finger picks upward on the 1st string

Here's what the forward roll looks like on the G and D7 chords in TAB notation:

G   D7

Note: The thumb almost never picks upward on the 5th string.

Practice the roll without worrying about the song. You can hear the roll on the accompanying recording. Once you get comfortable with the roll pattern, begin to move some of the fingers around. For example, use the index finger to play the 3rd string instead of the 2nd string, and use the thumb on the 4th string instead of always picking the 5th string.

Introducing the Accent

Track 13

The symbol > means to emphasize the note to which it's attached.

> >
Play a little louder.

Rhythm

There is usually a strong emphasis on the first beat of each eighth-note sequence. Listen to the roll on the recording.

Although the rhythm of the rolls is usually written like this

the pattern sounds more like this:

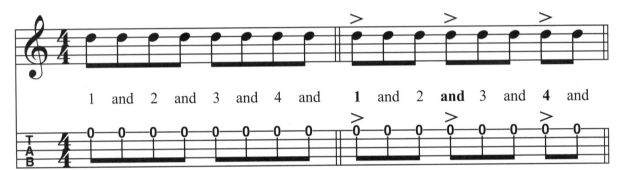

Standard Notation

1 and 2 and 3 and 4 and   **1** and 2 **and** 3 and **4** and

Tablature

Right-Hand Position

Refer back to the position of the right hand that was covered on page 10. Bluegrass players usually rest the pinky finger just above the bridge. Other players rest both fingers but if that isn't suitable to your hand, or seems uncomfortable, rest either the little finger or the ring finger. Resting your finger on the head of the

banjo provides stability as you play the rolls. In a short time, you will be playing quite rapidly, so this stability is critical for developing right-hand technique.

You should bend the right-hand fingers so that they are ready to attack the strings. See photo below.

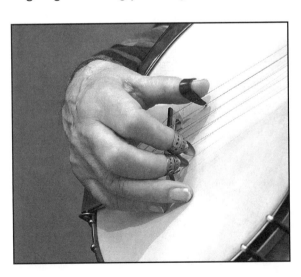

Right hand with thumb and finger picks slightly bent and in position to play a roll.

You're now ready to play "Tom Dooley" on the following page with the forward roll. The trick is to be able to continue the roll and to change the chord without slowing down. The best way to accomplish this is to get so familiar with the fingerboard that you can change to the D7 chord without looking at the neck of the banjo.

TOM DOOLEY (VERSION 2)

Track 14

Moderately

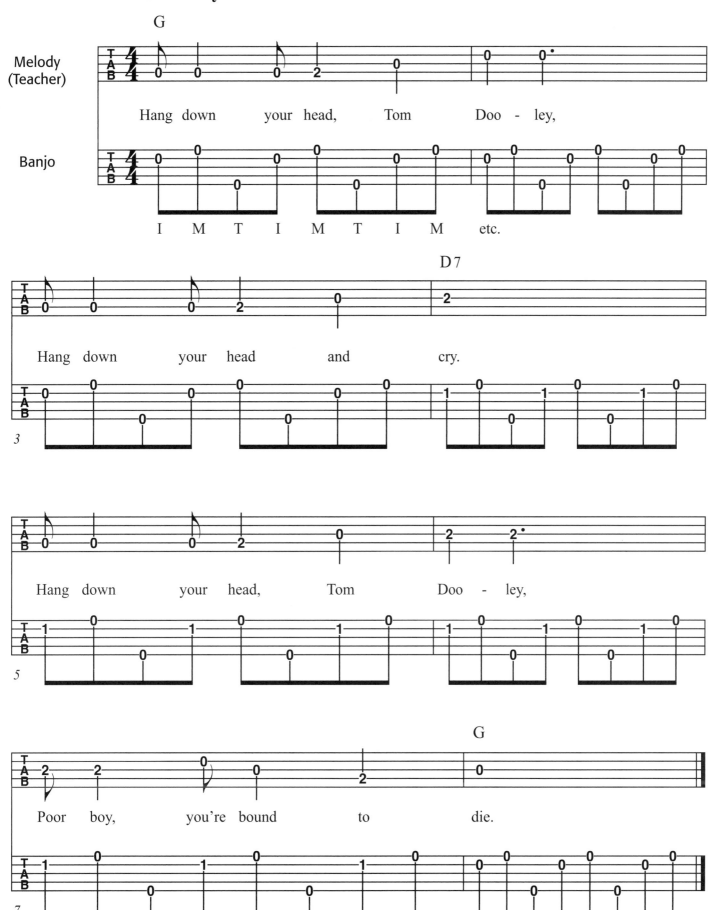

Forward Roll Variations

Now that you've gotten your feet wet with the roll, try moving
your fingers around a bit. Let's begin with the index finger.
Instead of playing in the 2nd–1st–5th–2nd–1st–5th–2nd–1st
string sequence, play 2nd–1st–5th–3rd–1st–5th–2nd–1st as
shown in Example 1 below.

Forward Roll Example 1

Track 15.1

You can also experiment by occasionally moving the thumb to the 4th string, and finally
by moving the 1st finger to the 3rd string, followed by the middle finger to the 2nd string,
as shown in Examples 2 and 3 below.

Forward Roll Example 2

Track 15.2

Forward Roll Example 3

Track 15.3

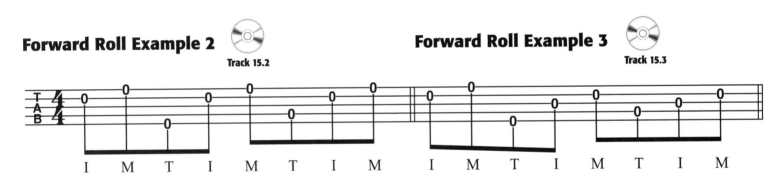

Your goal is to be able to make these right-hand movements without actually
looking at the strings, in the same way that you were able to master changing from
the G to the D7 chord without looking at the banjo.

Other Songs

There are many songs that only require you to play two chords. Here are a few that
can be played using only G and D7:

"Skip to My Lou"

"Polly Wolly Doodle"

"Old Blue"

"He's Got the Whole World in His Hands"

"Go Tell Aunt Rhody"

"Billy Boy"

"Achy Breaky Heart"

"Buffalo Gals"

"Pick a Bale o' Cotton"

"Wheels on the Bus"

"Yellow Rose of Texas"

Try using any of these tunes to practice the forward roll until it becomes second nature.

The C Chord

 **Track 16.1**

Once you learn how to play the C chord, a whole new world will open up. There are thousands of songs that can played using only these three chords: G, D7, and C.

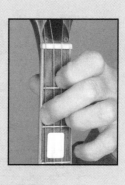

The C chord requires the use of three fingers, so it's a bit more difficult to play than D7. Start by practicing changing chords. First use only the right thumb to brush down across the strings. Play:

G / / / | G / / / | G / / / | G / / / | C / / / | C / / / | C / / / | C / / / |

G / / / | G / / / | G / / / | G / / / ‖

 **Track 16.2**

Next, try:

G / / / | G / / / | G / / / | G / / / | C / / / | C / / / | C / / / | C / / / |

G / / / | G / / / | G / / / | G / / / | D7 / / / | D7 / / / | G / / / | G / / / ‖

Track 16.3

Be sure to practice slowly enough so that you can change chords without hesitating or slowing down. If you find yourself unable to do this, slow the tempo down till you can.

G / / / | G / / / | G / / / | G / / / | C / / / | C / / / | C / / / | C / / / |

D7 / / / | D7 / / / | G / / / | G / / / ‖

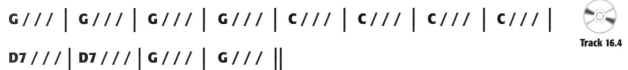 **Track 16.4**

Next, try to play the forward roll while changing the chords. Try the sequence:

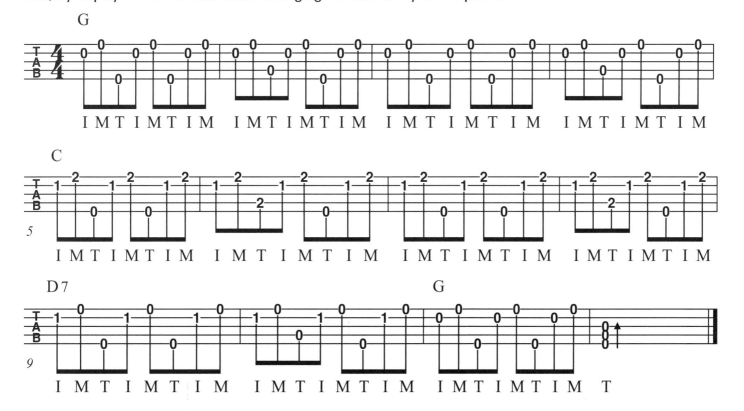

Now you're ready for our next song, "The Roving Gambler."

THE ROVING GAMBLER 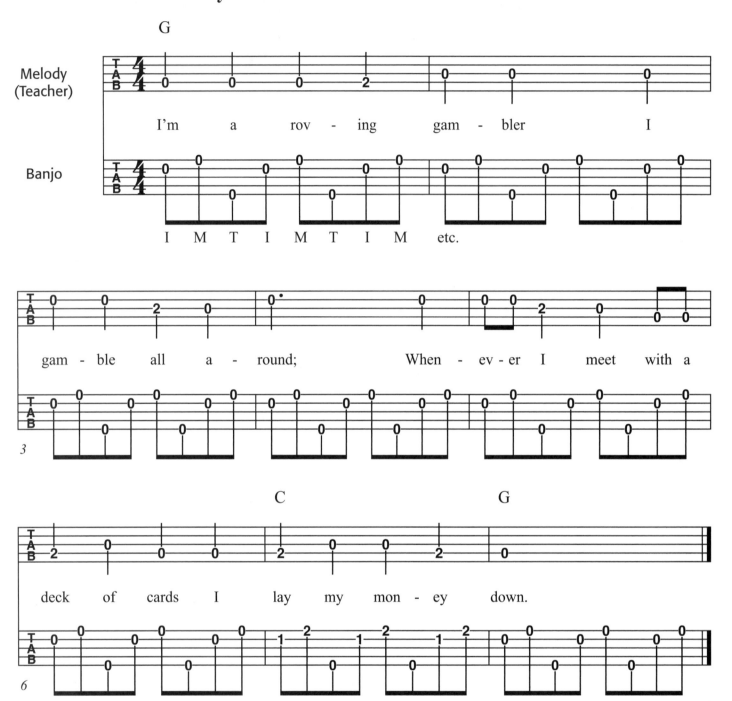 Track 17

This song features two chords, G and C, and uses the forward roll.

Moderately

Adjusting the Rolls to Find the Melody

Playing rolls is great fun, and in a short time, you should be able to play at a fairly rapid tempo. However, melodies don't necessarily fit precisely into the patterns, and you'll need to make a variety of adjustments to coordinate the melody with the rolls. Look at the melody of "The Roving Gambler" and you'll notice the first few notes are on the 4th string. You can at least imply the melody in your accompaniment by adjusting the roll so that the index finger plays the 4th string, while the middle finger plays the 3rd string. For the second measure of the music, move the index finger over to the 3rd string, then play the 2nd string with the middle finger.

Experiment with moving the right-hand fingers around. Next, we'll introduce the backward roll.

The Backward Roll

Track 18

Start with the 1st string, and work backward across the strings. The sequence is:

1. Middle finger picks up on 1st string
2. Thumb picks down on 5th string
3. Index finger picks up on 2nd string
4. Middle finger picks up on 1st string
5. Thumb picks down on 5th string
6. Index finger picks up on 2nd string
7. Middle finger picks up on 1st string
8. Thumb picks down on 5th string

THE ROVING GAMBLER (VERSION 2)

Below is the TAB for "The Roving Gambler" using the backward roll.

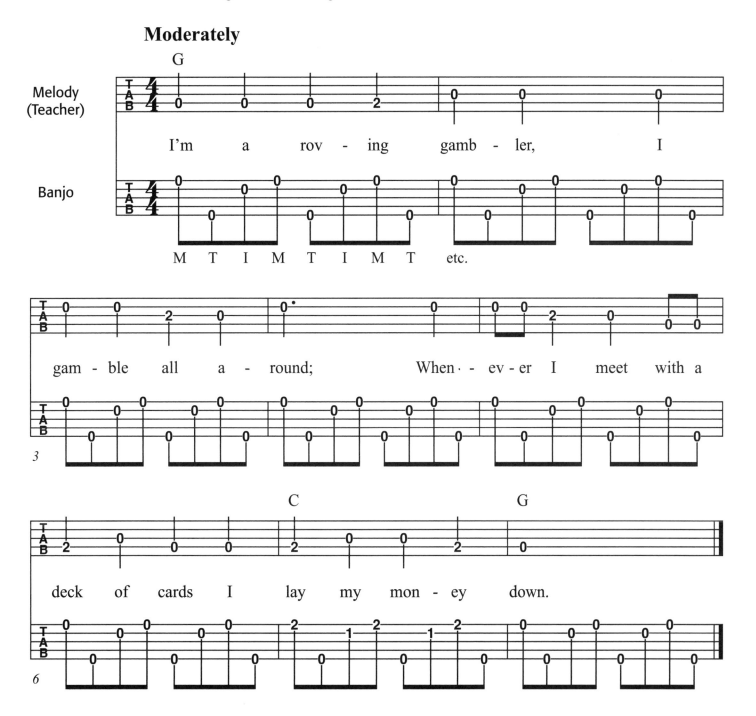

The Forward-Backward Roll (Thumb Leads)

One of the most useful rolls in bluegrass is the *forward-backward roll.* It's called the forward-backward roll because the first three notes go forward across the banjo from the low strings to the high strings, then the 4th to 6th notes move backward in the opposite direction. Here's how to do it:

1. Thumb plays 3rd or 4th string (alternate between the two)

2. Index finger picks upward on the 2nd string

3. Middle finger picks upward on the 1st string

4. Thumb plays 5th string

5. Middle finger picks upward on the 1st string

6. Index finger picks upward on the 2nd string

7. Thumb plays either the 3rd or 4th string

8. Index finger picks upward on the 2nd string

Here's how the forward-backward roll looks on the G and D7 chords:

Track 19

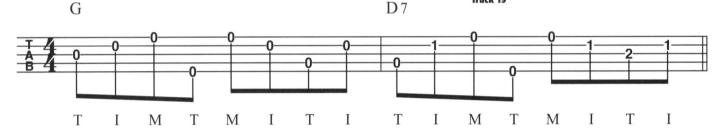

Introducing the Pickup

Not every piece of music begins on beat 1. Music sometimes begins with an incomplete measure called an *upbeat,* or *pickup.* If the pickup has just one beat, the last measure will have only three beats in $\frac{4}{4}$ or one beat in $\frac{2}{4}$. "Goin' Down the Road Feelin' Bad" starts on the fourth beat of the measure. Before you begin the roll, play the G chord by brushing down or up across the strings. You can do this by using the pinch, which might entail playing the 4th string with the thumb while the index finger plays the 2nd string, or brush down across the strings with your ring finger (the one that isn't wearing the pick), or brush back across the strings with your thumb, starting with the 1st string.

As you proceed through the book, you will learn more and more ways to adapt the roll to different melodies.

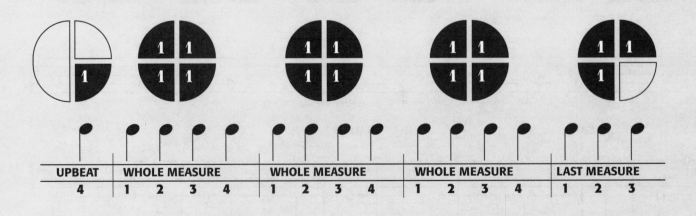

GOIN' DOWN THE ROAD FEELIN' BAD

This is a traditional blues tune. Get familiar with it and then we'll show you how to play the forward-backward roll.

Cut Time

This symbol ¢ indicates *cut time*, meaning the time value is cut in half. Half notes will receive 1 beat, quarter notes half a beat, etc. Cut time looks the same as $\frac{4}{4}$ but is played with a two-beat feel.

Moderately

Track 20

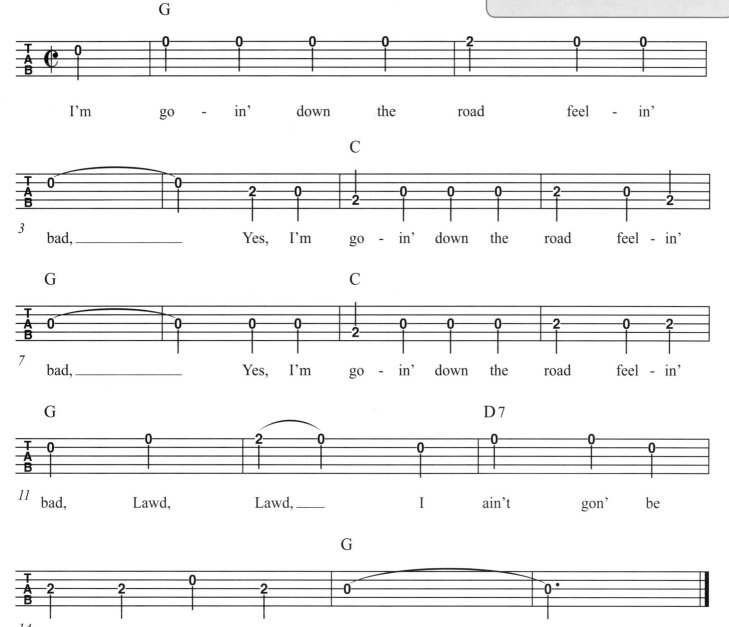

Additional Lyrics

I lost the only girl I ever had (repeat three times)
And I ain't goin' to be treated this a-way.

Goin' where those chilly winds don' blow (three times)
And I ain't goin' to be treated this a-way

Goin' where the water tastes like wine (3x)
And I ain't goin' to be treated this a-way

City water tastes like turpentine (3x)
And I ain't goin' to be treated this a-way

GOIN' DOWN THE ROAD FEELIN' BAD (VERSION 2)

With forward-backward roll

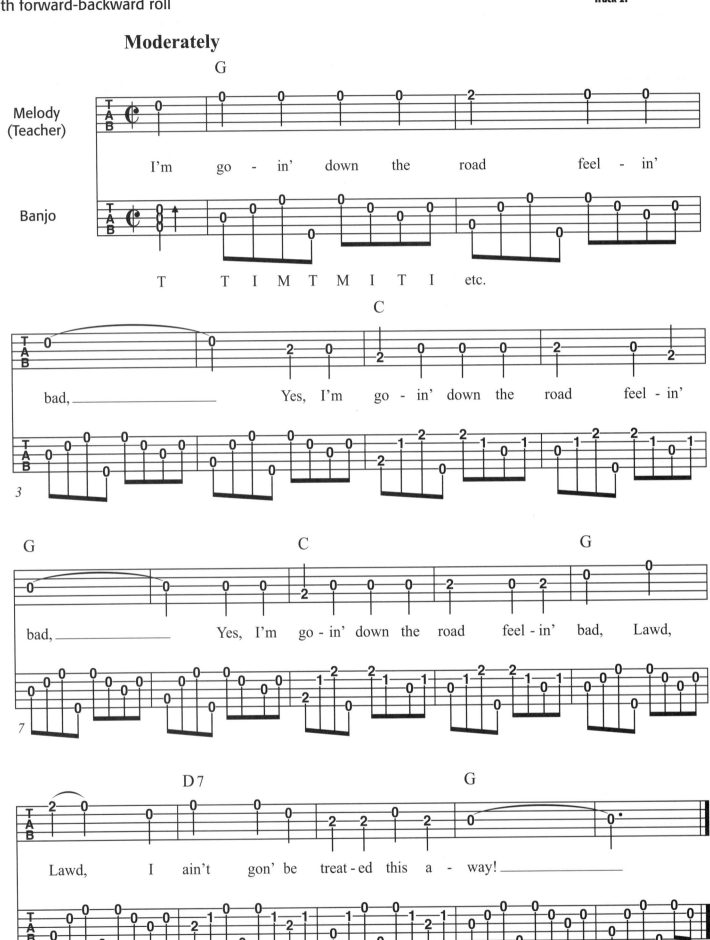

Goin' Down the Road Feelin' Bad (Version 3)

Track 22

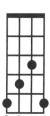

G^{III}

3 2 1 4

Here's another solo that mixes various rolls. When you see "GIII," use the alternate G chord on the right. This alternate way to play the G chord has a rough quality that is appropriate for the so-called "high, lonesome sound." You can use it in place of the open-string G chord anytime it sounds right to you. The "III" means the chord is played at the 3rd fret. Also, notice the last note in the song is played with the thumb alone.

Moderately

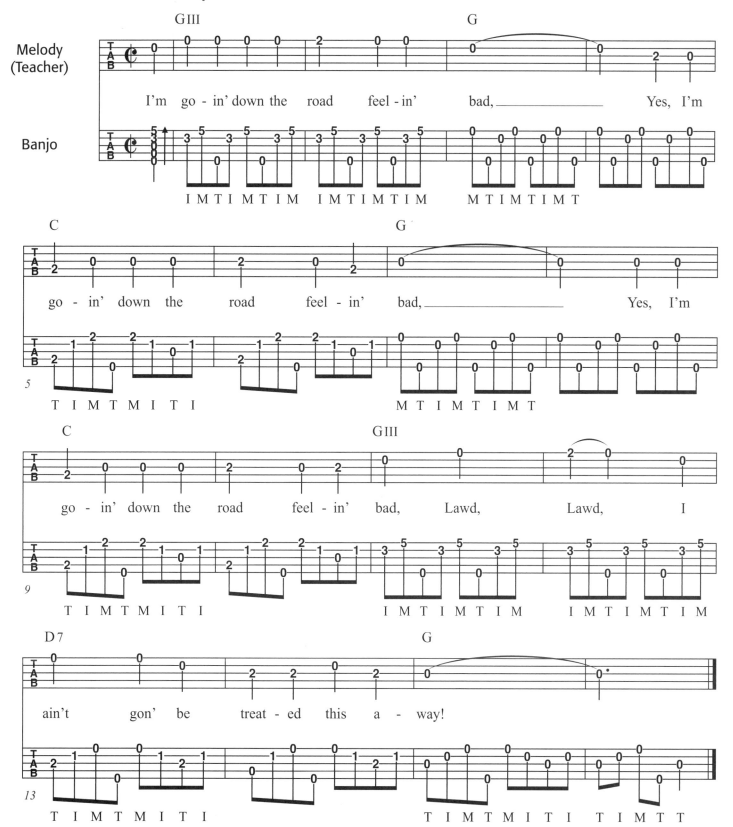

The Hammer-On

Track 23

It is possible to play notes with the left hand without using the right hand to pick them. This technique is called *hammering-on.*

Start with the D7 chord. Lift your left hand off the 3rd string at the 2nd fret, then, using the right-hand thumb, play the 3rd string open. With the middle finger of the left hand come down on the 2nd fret of the 3rd string almost immediately. You should hear both notes clearly.

If you're not hearing both notes with equal strength, it means that you have either waited too long to use the left-hand finger, or possibly you have used that finger too quickly. The motion should be smooth and even. The hammer-on note is designated by the small circle O in the diagram and by an H in the right-hand fingering.

Once this becomes familiar to you, do the same thing with the 2nd string at the 1st fret. Pick the note with your right index finger.

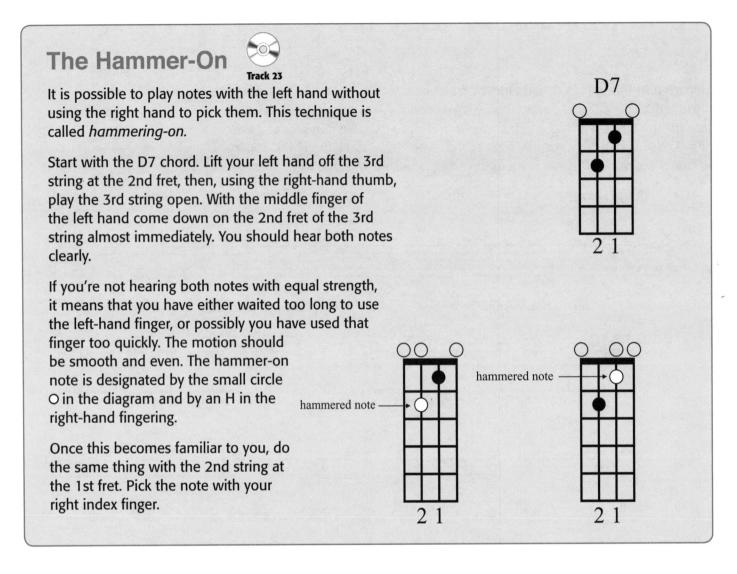

When you are comfortable with these hammer-ons, do them successively; first try the 3rd string then the 2nd. Listen to the recording to hear how it sounds when you have mastered it.

Try the bluegrass roll below, which combines the hammer-on with the roll.

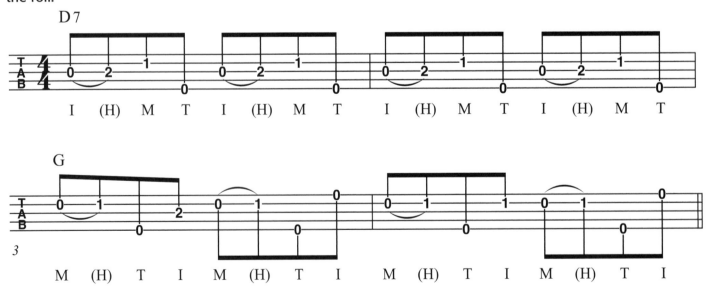

Why Hammer On?

One of the things hammering-on will enable you to do is to play melody notes that are not in the chord. We'll cover that shortly.

Hammer-Ons with the C Chord

Track 24

The diagram to the right is the C chord you have already learned.

Similar to what you did with the D7 chord, hammer on each of the chord notes as shown below:

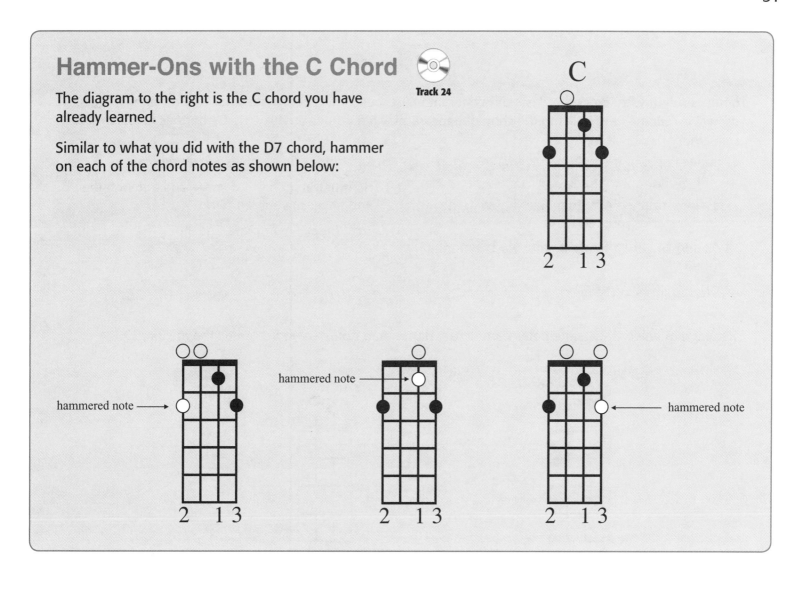

Try this bluegrass roll with C-chord hammer-ons below.
Remember, in TAB, the letter H means that note is a hammer-on.

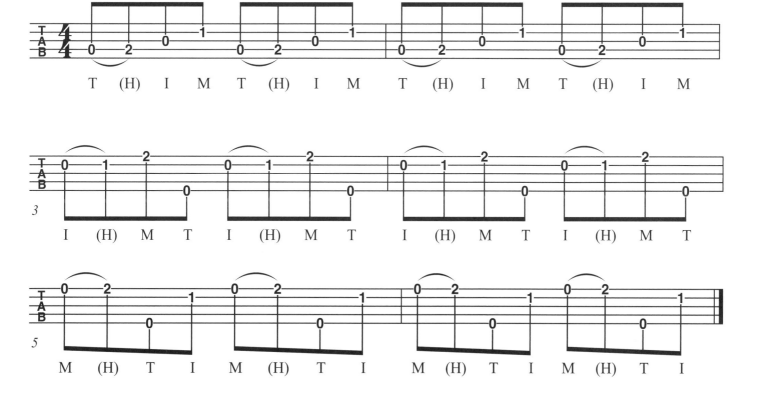

32

Hammer-Ons with the G Chord

Track 25

Hammering-on with the G chord is a different matter. Because the G chord does not use left-hand fingers, you will be adding new notes to the chord when you play a hammer-on. Play the G chord as follows:

1. Index finger of the right hand plays the open 2nd string

2. Hammer on the 4th string, 2nd fret with the 2nd finger of your left hand

3. Middle finger of the right hand plays 1st string open

4. Thumb plays 5th string open

5. Right Index finger plays 3rd string open

6. Hammer on at the 3rd string 2nd fret with the 2nd finger of your left hand

7. Right Index finger plays 2nd string

8. Thumb plays 5th string

The diagram below shows the notes hammered. Hammered notes are indicated by the marking O.

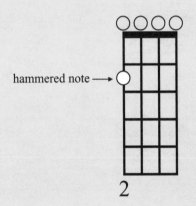
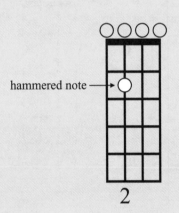

In TAB notation, it looks like this:

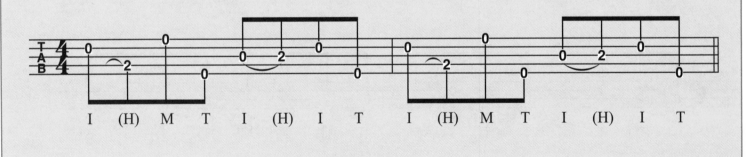

PLAYING TIP

You will need to apply a bit more pressure in the left hand when you hammer on notes that are not fingered with the right hand. If you are not getting a good, clear sound, you are probably either moving too quickly or too slowly, or you are not exerting enough force with the left hand.

Listen to the recording to get a clear idea of what the hammered notes should sound like.

HAWTHORNE HAMMERS Track 26

Below is a short piece that combines rolls with hammer-ons on the G, C, and D7 chords. Practice this slowly until you are comfortable playing it at a reasonable tempo. On the recording, we've played this example at a very slow tempo, and then at a medium tempo.

Notice that not every sequence of four notes uses hammer-ons. In the next-to-last measure, the roll is broken up by continuous hammer-ons. The last note is a single note that gets two beats.

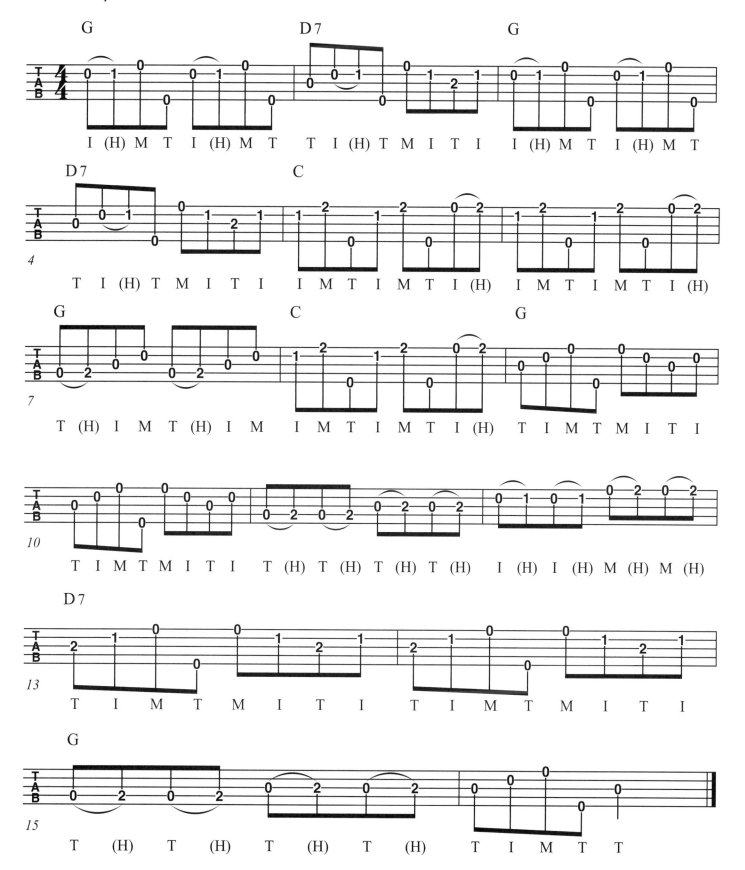

The Capo

A *capo* (KAY-po or KAH-po) is a plastic or metal device that you can place across the strings to raise the key of a song.

Capo across the 2nd fret .

small nail

"Railroad spikes"

5th string capo in position.

Railroad Spikes

After the capo is in position, for example across the 2nd fret, you will have to re-tune the 5th string. This string can be raised as much as two notes from a G up to an A, but it probably won't go any higher without breaking. Banjo players have developed two solutions for this problem. One is to place "railroad spikes" (small nails that look like miniatures of the real thing) in various higher frets (see above). When you want to change the key, simply place the 5th string under the spikes and it will go up in pitch without any problems.

Sliding Capo

Another solution is to use a sliding 5th-string capo that goes up the neck. If you want to raise the 5th string to an A, simply slide the capo up to the 7th fret. In this way, the 5th string will sound an A, not a G. This capo is often known as a "Shubb capo," after Rick Shubb, the leading manufacturer of these devices. If you're in an actual playing situation and need to make a key change in the middle of a song, the Shubb capo is superior to railroad spikes, as it is much faster and easier to use. Whichever capo you prefer, it's best to have a professional repair person install it and show you how to use it.

Placing the capo across the strings may have the unintended effect of knocking the instrument slightly out of tune. Sometimes this calls for touching up the tuning of all the strings.

Note: You may find the sound of the 5th string is slightly muted when you use a capo. There may even be some sort of unpleasant buzz if you're playing particularly hard. This is a common occurrence, so do not worry that you've made some sort of mistake.

Here is a list of keys for a banjo in G tuning with the capo at frets 1 through 5:

Capo across 1st fret	Banjo is in the key of A♭
Capo across 2nd fret	Banjo is in the key of A
Capo across 3rd fret	Banjo is in the key of B♭
Capo across 4th fret	Banjo is in the key of B
Capo across 5th fret	Banjo is in the key of C

For now, you should get used to using the capo on the 2nd fret. You'll need to re-tune the 5th string to an A. (Match the sound of the 1st string at the 7th fret.) An electronic tuner will come in handy here, because if you don't have one, you may end up tuning too high and might even break the 5th string.

The reason you'll often use the capo at the 2nd fret is because fiddle players prefer the keys of D and A, and the key of A for the banjo is accomplished with the capo at the 2nd fret.

The F and G7 Chords

Track 27

Playing in the key of D is another matter. You can stay in the same G tuning, but you will need the C, F, and G7 chords in the key of D. You already know the C chord, so the F and G7 chords are shown to the right. Notice that the F chord requires you to use four fingers of the left hand. This will take you a while to get used to, but it isn't really difficult.

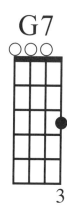

CAPO REVIEW **Track 28**

When you play the G, C, and D7 chords in the key of A with the capo at the 2nd fret, they sound like A, D, and E7.

When you play the C, F, and G7 chords in the key of D with the capo at the 2nd fret, they sound like D, G, and A7.

About Capo Notation

In capo notation, Roman numerals are used to indicate at what fret the capo should be placed. In addition to where the capo should be placed, capo notation also indicates what the new note for the 5th string is. For example, "Capo II, ⑤ = A," means to place your capo at the 2nd fret. When the capo is at the 2nd fret, the open 5th string needs to be an A note.

To the right is quick Roman numeral review.

Roman Numerals	
I or i................1	V or v............5
II or ii............2	VI or vi...........6
III or iii...........3	VII or vii........7
IV or iv...........4	

For the next few tunes, try to find a fiddler or mandolinist to play with you, or play with the available recording, which has both fiddle and banjo.

RED RIVER VALLEY*
Track 29

This song is actually in the key of A, but you will be playing it in G with a capo at the 2nd fret. When you read the tablature, think of the capo as if it were the nut of the banjo, ignoring the part of the neck that is behind the capo. Don't forget to tune the 5th string two frets higher up to an A.

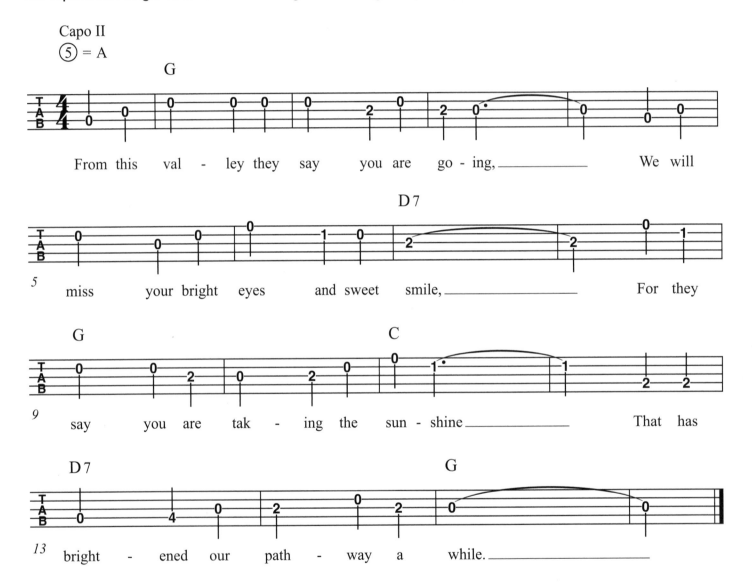

Additional Lyrics

*Come and sit by my side if you love me
Do not hasten to bid me adieu
Just remember the Red River Valley,
And that girl who has loved you so true.*

*From this valley they say you are going,
When you leave, may your darling go too?
Would you leave her behind, unprotected,
When she loves no one else there, but you.*

*Note: This song was written about the Red River in Canada, not the one in Texas.

RED RIVER VALLEY (SOLO)

Track 30

Banjo solo

Below is the solo for "Red River Valley" with hammer-ons. Notice the first two notes are played alone before you start the rolls. Every once in a while, the rolls stop so the melody is played as individual notes.

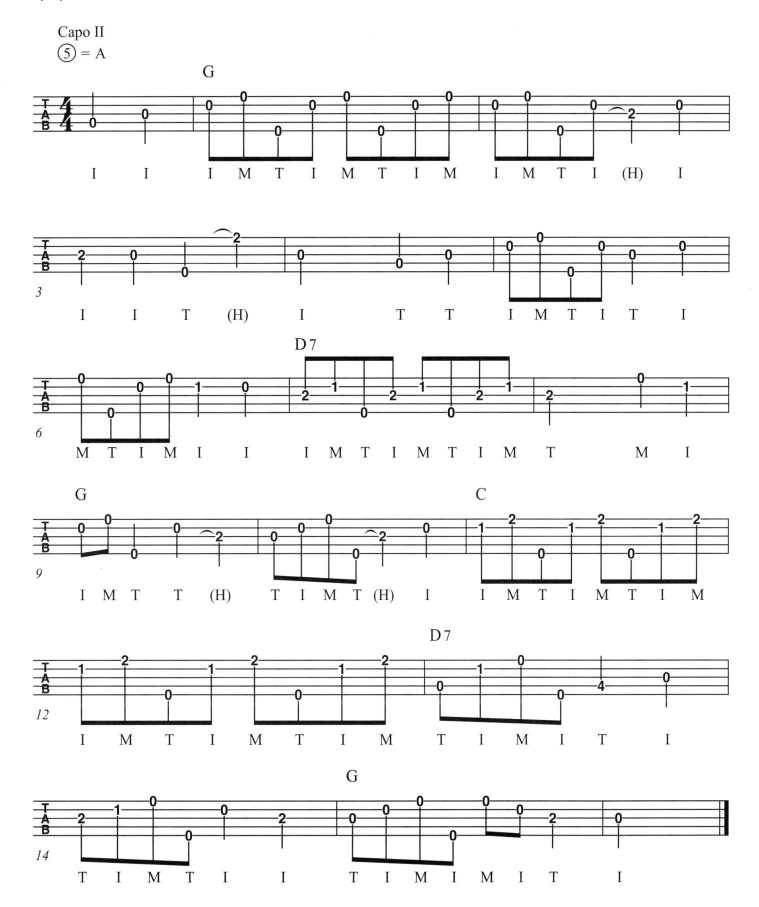

The Key of D

To play in the key of D, keep your capo at the 2nd fret. You will be fingering in the key of C, but with the capo at the 2nd fret, you'll actually sound in D. Don't forget to tune your 5th string two frets higher to an A.

To the right are the three chords you'll need:

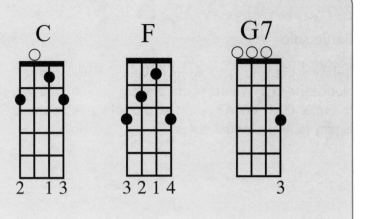

HARD, AIN'T IT HARD

Track 31

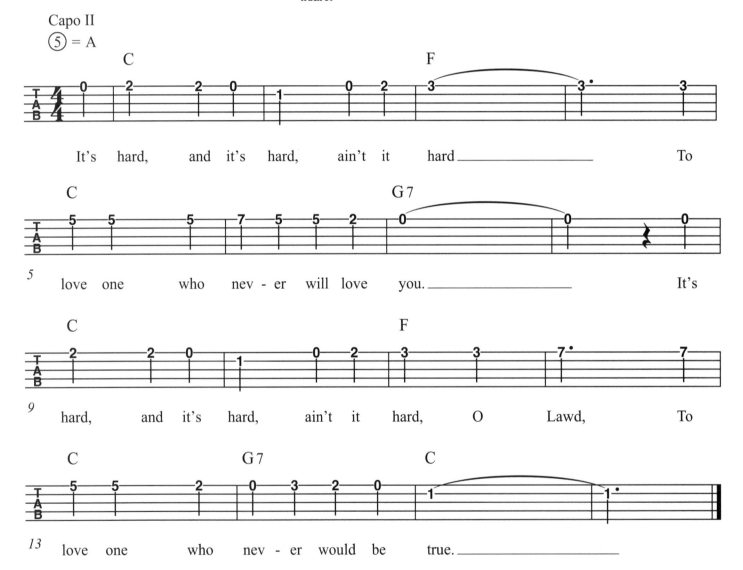

Capo II
⑤ = A

It's hard, and it's hard, ain't it hard _____ To

love one who nev - er will love you. _____ It's

hard, and it's hard, ain't it hard, O Lawd, To

love one who nev - er would be true. _____

Additional Lyrics

There is a place in this old town,
That's where my true love lays around,
He takes other women, right down on his knee,
And he tells them a little tale he won't tell me.

Don't go to drinking and a gamblin',
Don't go there your sorrows to drown,
That hard liquor place is a lowdown disgrace,
It's the meanest old place in this town.

Hard, Ain't It Hard (Version 2)

Track 32

Banjo solo

Before attempting this solo, make sure your capo is in place across
the 2nd fret and that the 5th string is tuned up to an A.

Capo II
⑤ = A

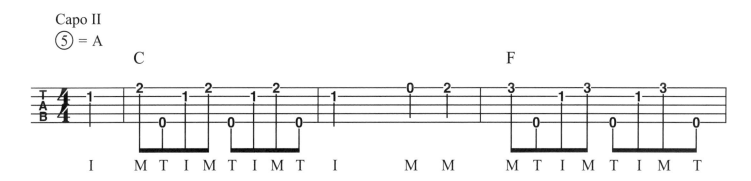

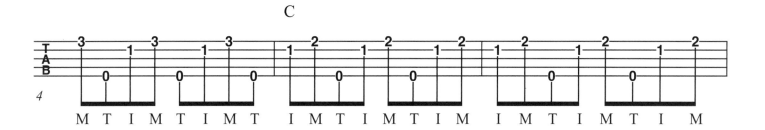

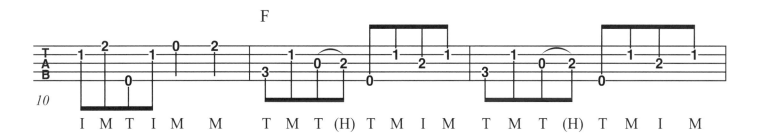

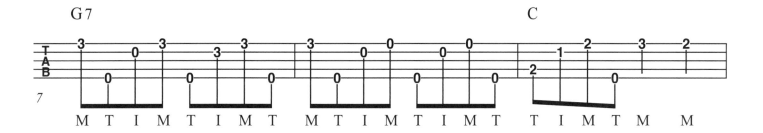

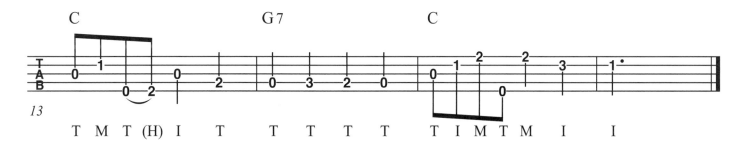

The E Minor Chord

To the right is a diagram of the E minor chord. Practice changing back and forth between the Em and G chords.

Since this song is too low to sing in the key of G, use the capo at the 2nd fret. This means—while you'll be fingering in the key of G—you will actually be sounding in the key of A. Also, remember to tune your 5th string up to A.

RED APPLE JUICE

Track 33

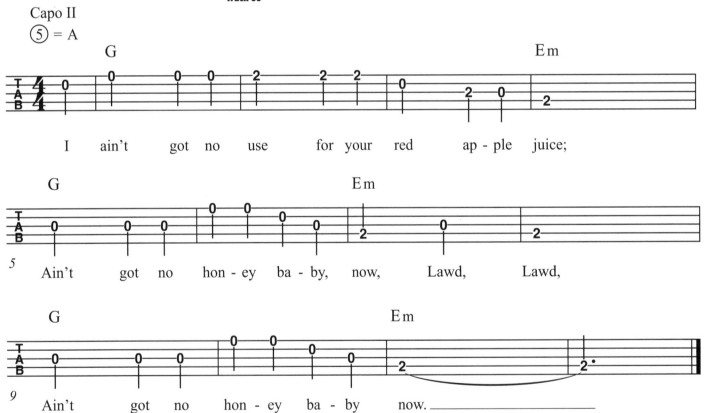

Capo II
⑤ = A

G ... Em
I ain't got no use for your red ap-ple juice;

G ... Em
Ain't got no hon-ey ba-by, now, Lawd, Lawd,

G ... Em
Ain't got no hon-ey ba-by now.____

Additional Lyrics

*Who'll rock this cradle, and who'll sing this song?
Who's gonna love me when I'm gone, Lawd, Lawd,
Who's gonna love me when I'm gone.*

*I've done all I could do, to try and get along with you,
Still you're not satisfied, Lawd, Lawd,
Still, you're not satisfied.*

*Lay in the shade, with every dime I made,
What more could a poor boy do, Lawd, Lawd,
What more could a poor boy do?*

*I ain't got no use, for your red rockin' chair,
Ain't got no honey baby there,
Ain't got no honey baby there.*

The E Minor Chord with a Hammer-On

To the right are diagrams of the E minor chord with the hammered notes marked with an O. Practice this hammer-on, then play the solo for "Red Apple Juice."

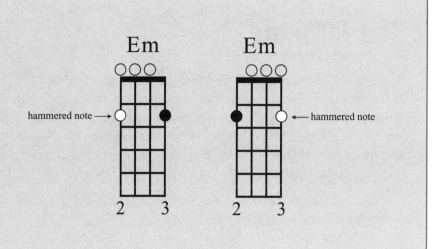

"Red Apple Juice" uses the forward-backward roll.

RED APPLE JUICE (VERSION 2)

Banjo solo

Track 34

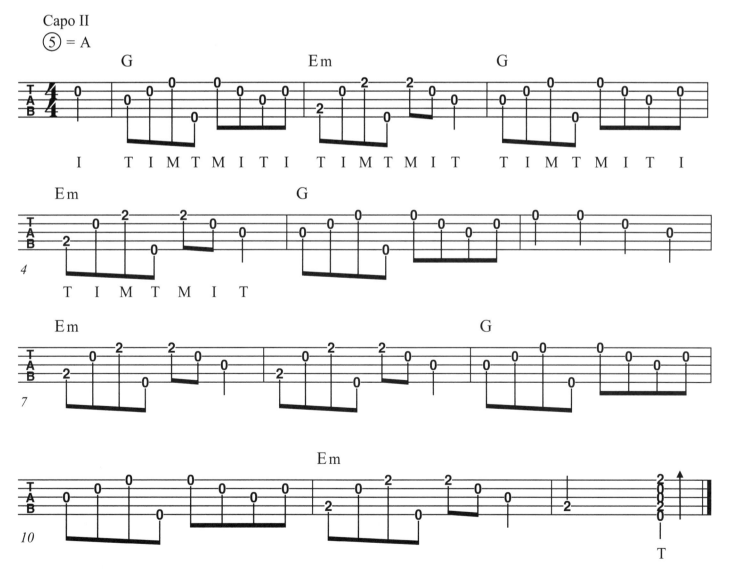

Try experimenting with the E minor chord, hammering on at the 4th string, 2nd fret.

The D Chord

D

"Feelin' Lonesome" is an original piece by Dick Weissman that features hammer-ons using the GIII chord at the 3rd fret. (Don't forget to remove the capo.) We'll be adding the D chord to your chord vocabulary. Although we've shown it with the 4th string open, the D chord can also be fingered with the ring finger of the left hand playing the 4th string at the 4th fret.

We've included a chord diagram for GIII to remind you of the fingering.

3 1 2 4

FEELIN' LONESOME

 Track 35

GIII

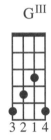

3 2 1 4

You can arrange this piece in your own style. For example, try adding hammer-ons where there are none and taking out the ones in the solo.

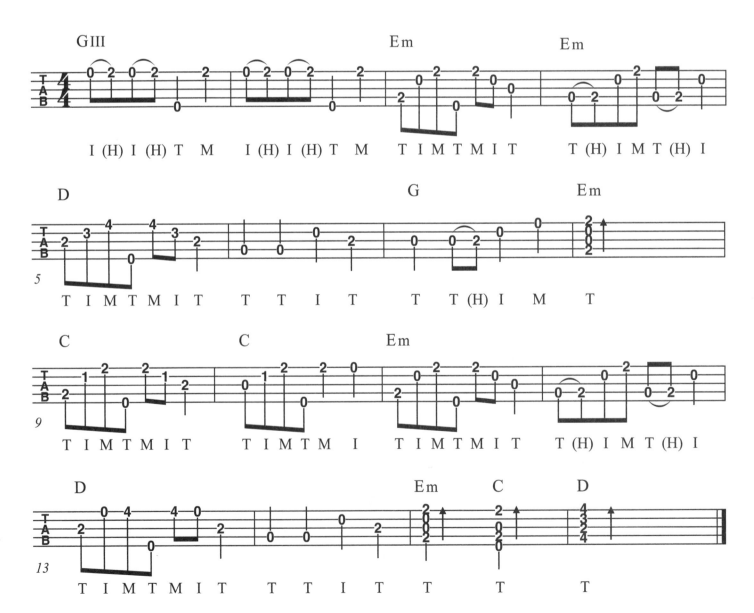

The Alternate F Chord

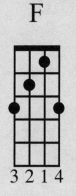

Let's add one more chord to your arsenal. To the right is the F chord. Notice that it is the same as the full GIII chord from the previous page, but moved down two frets.

3 2 1 4

Pull-Off

The *pull-off* (P) consists of the left hand actually picking a note.

Dotted Quarter Note

A *dotted quarter note* lasts 1½ beats, which is the same as a quarter note tied to an eighth note.

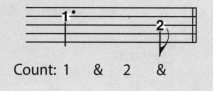

Count: 1   &   2   &

Since "Little Maggie" is in $\frac{2}{4}$ time, there are only two beats in each measure. The pull-off occurs when the left hand fingers a string in two places. In this case, the ring finger is at the 3rd fret of the 2nd string, and the 1st finger is at the 1st fret of the 2nd string. When the ring finger pivots off the string and the new note plays without using the right hand, it is called a pull-off.

LITTLE MAGGIE

Track 36

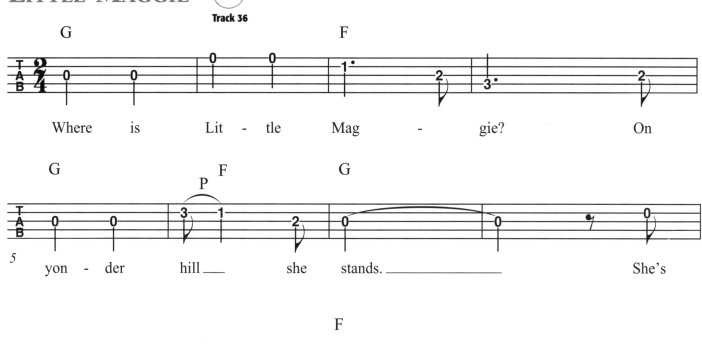

Little Maggie Solo Variations

The following pages introduce you to four solos for "Little Maggie." Various rolls and hammers have been incorporated into each solo.

Sixteenth Notes

"Little Maggie" features *sixteenth notes*. A sixteenth note is indicated by two flags or two beams and is half the length, or value, of an eighth note. So, two sixteenth notes equals one eighth note.

Count: 1 e & a

Little Maggie: Solo No. 1   Track 37.1

In the first solo, there are a number of places where the note D is played on the 3rd fret of the 2nd string, as well as the 1st string open. The very first note of the second measure is an example. The only slightly tricky part of "Little Maggie" is the change from G to F in the middle of the sixth measure of music.

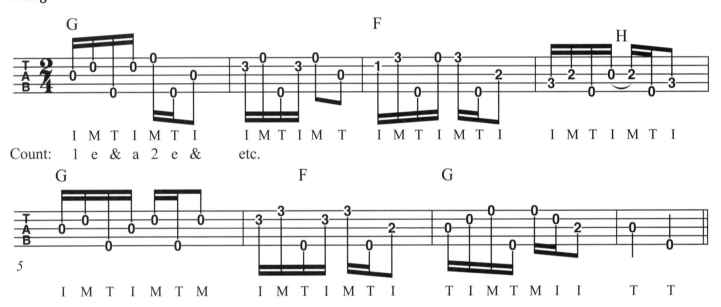

Little Maggie: Solo No. 2   Track 37.2

In solo number two, you will interrupt the roll in the sixth measure to make the chord change from G to F with single notes.

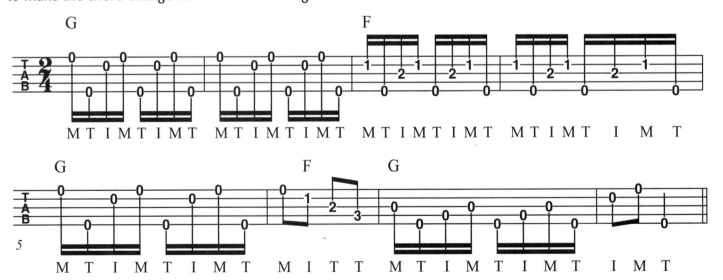

Little Maggie: Solo No. 3

Track 38.1

The third solo is very straightforward, with the thumb leading throughout.

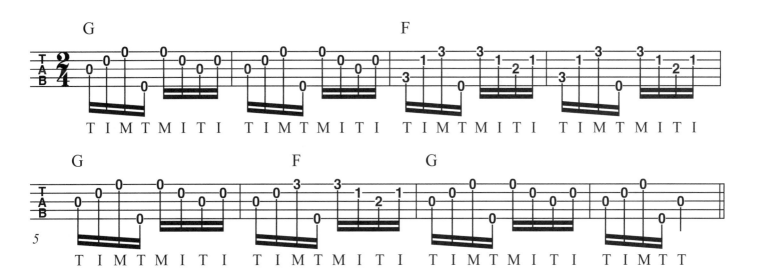

Little Maggie: Solo No. 4

Track 38.2

The final solo is a bit more difficult, as it combines pinches and rolls. The sixth measure features a string of single notes that are hammered on.

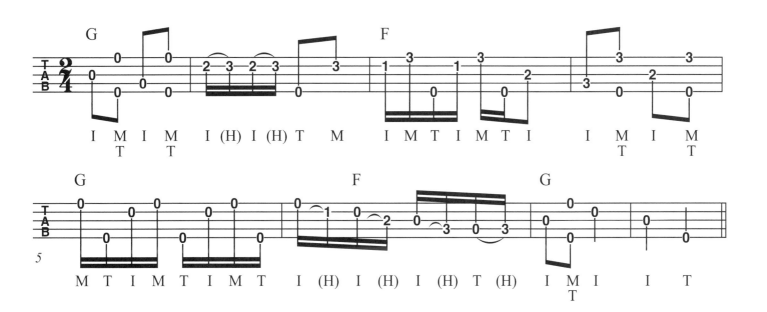

"Chords and Chords" incorporates all of the chords you have learned so far. It tests your ability to improvise as you are only given a series of chords, so it's up to you to make up your own pinches and hammer-ons. Play them with any rolls that you wish.

Here are the chords featured in "Chords and Chords":

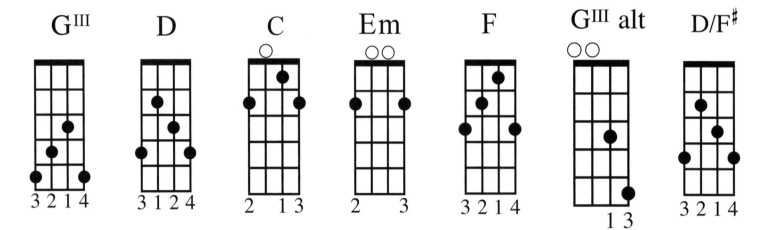

CHORDS AND CHORDS

This piece is in ⁴⁄₄ time, which means there are four beats in each measure. The slash marks mean to repeat the previous chord. For example, in the first measure, the GIII chord is played for four beats, once for the chord symbol and once each for the slash marks.

The roll you are using is played with two notes for every beat, so you'll actually be playing eight notes for each measure of four beats.

At the beginning of the piece, play the partial GIII chord, but in the 9th and 11th measures, simply drag the F chord up two frets to form a G chord.

Track 39

GIII / / /	D / / /	C / / /	G / / /
Em / / /	Em / / /	C / / /	Em / / /
F / / /	GIII / / /	F / / /	GIII / / /
D / / /	F / / /	D / / /	F / / /
D / / /	F / / /	D / / /	C / / /
G / / /	G / / /	F / / /	G / / / ‖

Note: Don't forget to interrupt the roll in any way that may seem appropriate every once in a while. Hearing an endless series of eighth notes can get tiresome.

$\frac{3}{4}$ Time

So far, everything you have played has been in either $\frac{2}{4}$ or $\frac{4}{4}$ time. Let's learn a new time signature now: $\frac{3}{4}$ time ("three-quarter time"), which is also referred to as *waltz time*. In $\frac{3}{4}$, there are three beats for each measure of music. Below are some right-hand bluegrass strums for playing in $\frac{3}{4}$ time. This new time signature is usually played very evenly, with a slight emphasis on the first beat of the measure.

$\frac{3}{4}$ Pinch

Track 40

Let's try a pinch in $\frac{3}{4}$ time. Follow these steps:

1. Your right-hand index finger plays the 3rd or 2nd string

2. Your right-hand middle finger plays the 1st string while the thumb plays the 5th string at the same time

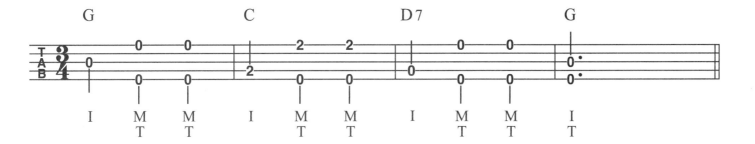

Below is another way to play in $\frac{3}{4}$ time with the pinch:

1. Your right-hand thumb plays the 4th or 5th string

2. Your right-hand index finger plays the 2nd string while the middle finger plays the 1st string at the same time

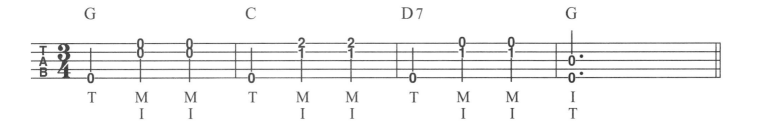

Playing the Strings Individually

Track 41

In the strum below, the roll is adapted for $\frac{3}{4}$ time. Instead of playing eight notes, you will now play six even notes.

1. Thumb plays the 3rd string

2. Index finger plays the 2nd string

3. Middle finger plays the 1st string

4. Thumb plays the 5th string

5. Index finger plays the 2nd string

6. Middle finger plays the 1st string

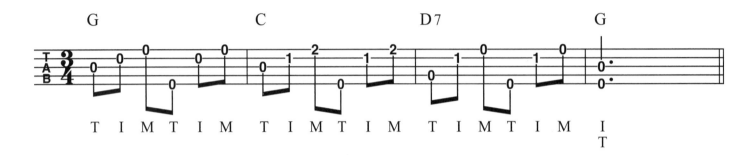

Variations

As with the bluegrass rolls you have already learned, you can change the sequence of the individual notes. For example, you could begin with the middle finger playing the 1st string and work backwards. Or you could begin with the index finger playing the 2nd string.

It is also possible to vary between playing the six individual notes and the pinches. A lot depends on the particular tune you are playing. There's a nice contrast between the two as the individual notes sound pleasant while the pinches produce a rougher sound. If you move your right hand away from the bridge, you can also get a more mellow sound, which may be appropriate for playing a waltz.

Introduction to "Down in the Valley"

On the following page is the melody for a beautiful old folk song called "Down in the Valley." First learn the melody, then we'll show you how to play the song with the $\frac{3}{4}$ strums you have just learned.

DOWN IN THE VALLEY

Track 42

> ## Introducing Quarter Rests
>
> We find the *quarter rest* ♩ in "Down in the Valley." A quarter rest (one beat of silence) is half the value of a half rest, so two quarter rests equals one half rest.

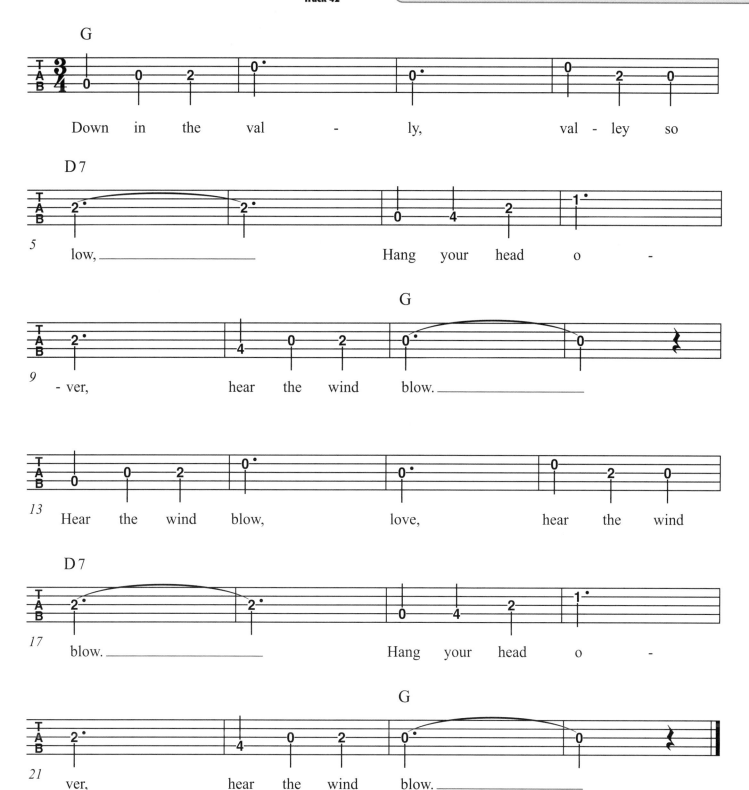

Additional Lyrics

If you don't love me, love whom you please,
Throw your arms 'round me, give my heart ease.
Give my heart ease, dear, give my heart ease,
Throw your arms 'round me, give my heart ease

Write me a letter, send it by mail;
Send it in care of Birmingham Jail.
Birmingham Jail, dear, Birmingham Jail.
Send it in care of Birmingham Jail.

This solo incorporates the pinch, individual notes, and the rolls
modified for ¾ time.

DOWN IN THE VALLEY (VERSION 2)

Track 43

Banjo solo

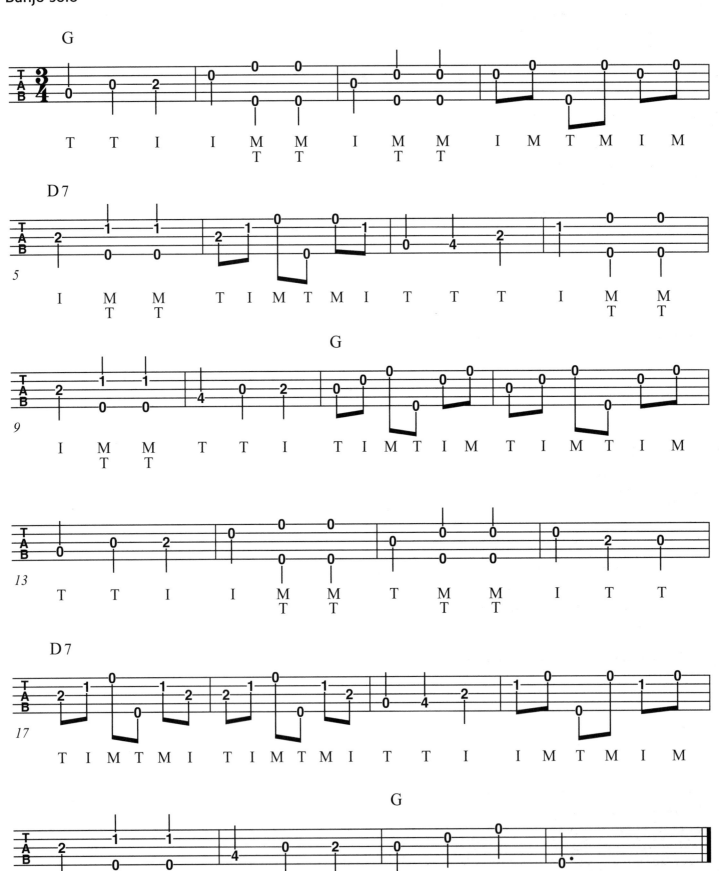

Backup Playing

There are a number of times when the banjo will play a backup role in a bluegrass band. One is during lead vocals, and another is when some other instrument is playing the solo part. The banjo is simply contributing to the rhythm section in these instances, rather than playing lead or solo.

Backup parts are often played up the neck of the banjo (that is, on the higher frets). These upper-register chords cut through the bluegrass ensemble with a more penetrating sound.

Alternate Chords

We've already covered the G chord at the 3rd fret. To the right are chord diagrams for the G, C, D, and D7 chords up the neck. For backup playing, it is sometimes best to use the D chord, and at other times the D7 chord. With this type of playing, the D and D7 chords are interchangeable.

When you play the C chord at the 5th fret, or the G chord at the 12th fret, you use only one left-hand finger, the index, across all four strings. This requires a bit more pressure than you have used in the left hand. Be sure your left-hand fretting finger is flat across the banjo neck, just behind (not on!) the fret. Take a look at the photo below for an example of how to do this.

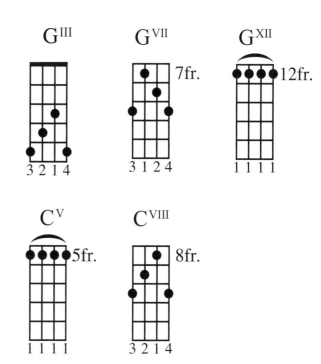

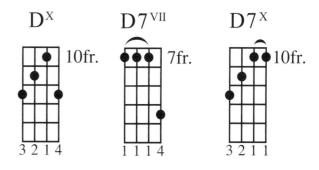

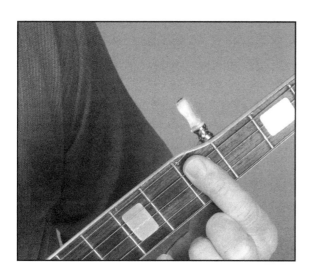

C chord at the 5th fret. Be sure your fretting-hand finger is flat across the neck and just behind the fret.

Backup Patterns

In $\frac{4}{4}$ time, backup patterns can be played on the 2nd and 4th beats of each measure. These beats are referred to as the *backbeats,* or *afterbeats.* In these instances, you do not play the 1st and 3rd beats.

Backup Pattern 1

In backup playing, the banjo will usually take a secondary role, playing the 2nd and 4th beats, while the fiddle, mandolin, or dobro take solos. Here's an example of what the banjo would play:

1st beat: Rest

2nd beat: Play

3rd beat: Rest

4th beat: Play

In TAB notation, it looks like this:

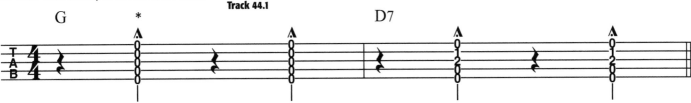

For these chords, it is common to use a *three-finger pinch,* with the right thumb, index, and middle fingers playing.

Backup Pattern 2

Here's another way to play backup. The rhythm for this pattern is two quarter notes, followed by four eighth notes, or long, long, short, short, short, short. Here it is in TAB notation:

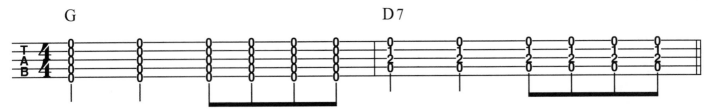

* This accent (∧) means to emphasize the chord and cut the sound off short.

It is also possible to add ties or rests into your backup playing. This produces more of a *syncopated,* or off-the-beat, feel. Below are three examples:

Backup Pattern Example 1

Track 45.1

Backup Pattern Example 2

Track 45.2

Backup Pattern Example 3

Track 45.3

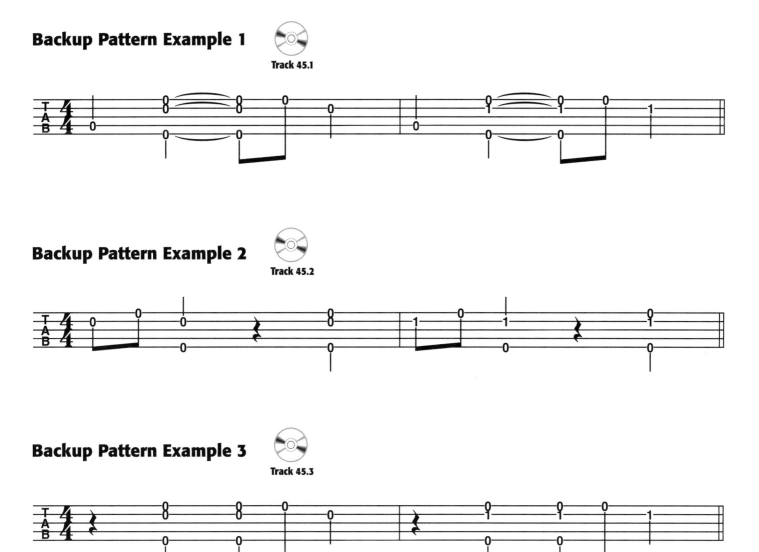

Listen to the available recording that includes the melody and the guitar playing rhythm. The guitar plays straight rhythm on the recording, while the banjo plays the offbeats.

Slides

The *slide* is a technique where a left-hand finger (or fingers) takes a note (or chord) and slides it up the neck of the banjo. For example, finger the D7 chord. After you've played the A note on the 3rd string at the 2nd fret, keep the pressure on the string and slide it up to the B note at the 4th fret on the same string. The slide is marked with a line connecting the two notes and the letters SL above.

Track 46.1

Next, try playing the following phrase:

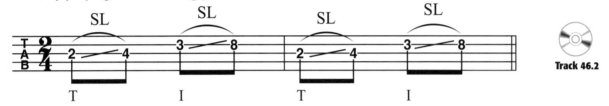

Track 46.2

Now, play the G chord. Take the middle finger of your left hand, and play the E note at the 4th string, 2nd fret, and slide it up to the G note at the 5th fret.

Track 46.3

Next, let's try playing a slide on GIII, followed by the notes indicated.

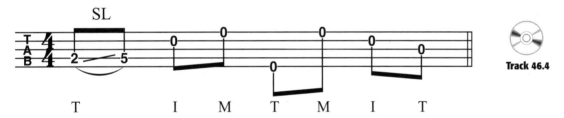

Track 46.4

Use the slide as an introduction to a song, or as a *vamp* (a repeated figure) between the verses of a song.

Play the G chord again. This time play the E on the 1st string at the 2nd fret and then slide it up to the G on the same string at the 5th fret.

Track 46.5

Finally, play the slide, as shown below.

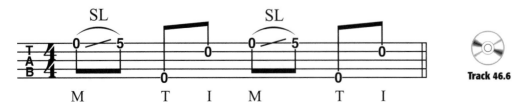

Track 46.6

Bending the Strings

Another technique to learn is *bending* a string with the left hand. When you bend, you are increasing the tension on a string, causing its pitch to rise. For example, take a look at the photo to the right. In it, you are grabbing the 3rd string at the 2nd fret and pulling it across the fingerboard. Bending is indicated by an upward curving arrow along with the amount of bend indicated in steps, or fractions of a step. When you bend 1/4 step, the note sounds halfway between the fingered note and the note one fret higher.

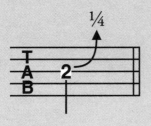

Track 47.1

Next, try bending the note twice, and then play the open G string. Play all the notes with the right thumb.

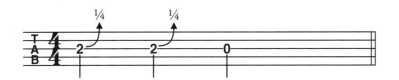

Track 47.2

This one is a good challenge: take the D7 chord and bend both of the fretted notes.

Track 47.3

Now bend the 3rd string at the 2nd fret, and then follow that by bending the 4th string at the 2nd fret.

Track 47.4

Finally, bend notes, then play the notes that follow without bending.

Now see if you can incorporate slides and bends into the pieces that you have already played.

C Tuning

Track 48.1

Along with the G tuning we've been using, another popular tuning for the banjo is the C tuning.

To get into the C tuning, tune the D string (the 4th string) down from a D to a C. You can use an electronic tuner, or you can do it by ear. If you do it by ear, the open 4th string is an octave lower than the C note at the 2nd string, 1st fret.

Or, the 4th string at the 7th fret is now the same note as the 3rd string open.

The four strings will now be tuned (reading from low to high): C, G, B, D. The 5th string remains tuned to G.

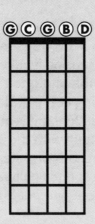

Here are the three basic chords in C tuning.

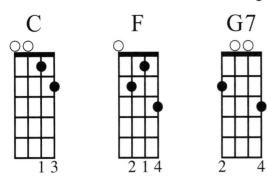

Below is the melody for the old blues song "Careless Love." Make sure your banjo is in C tuning before playing it.

CARELESS LOVE

Banjo in C Tuning

Track 48.2

Love,   oh love, oh care-less   love;   Love,   oh love, oh care-less   love;

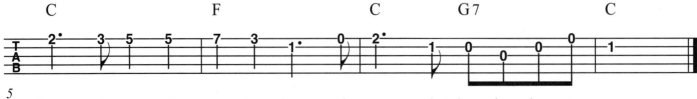

5

Love,   oh love, oh   care - less   love,   oh   see   what   love   has   done   to   me.

Below is a bluegrass-style solo for "Careless Love," using the C tuning. As you get used to the chords, try to incorporate hammer-ons. With the F chord, hammering on the 3rd string is especially effective. With G7, try hammering on the 4th string.

Since this is a blues song, try some bending as well, as that technique is always appropriate when playing the blues.

CARELESS LOVE (SOLO)

Track 49

Banjo solo

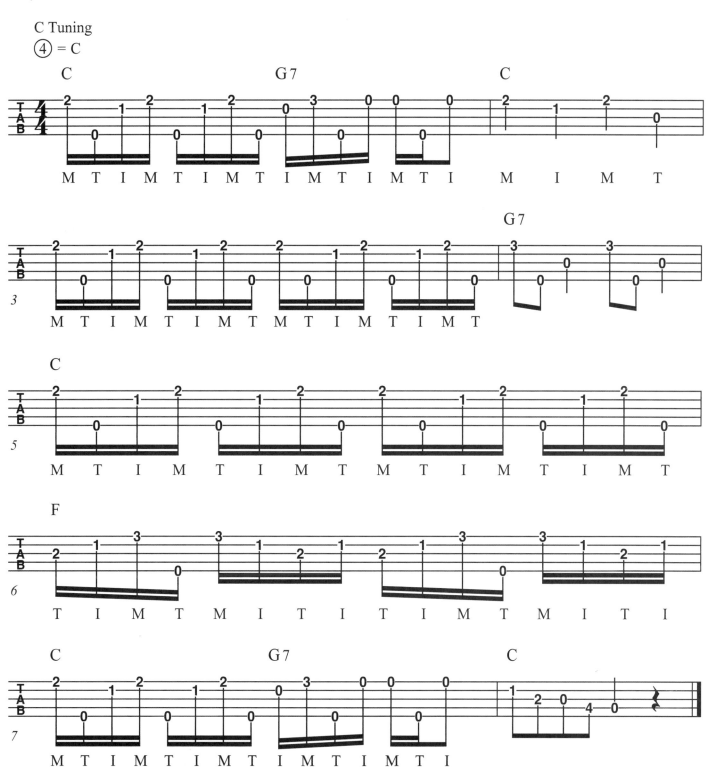

Congratulations, you have completed the method portion of *Alfred's Basic 5-String Banjo*, Book 1! Starting on the following page is an appendix that reviews chords and music notation, and provides additional information on banjo heads, strings, bridges, and fingerpicks.

Appendix

Chord Diagrams for Banjo in G Tuning: G D G B D

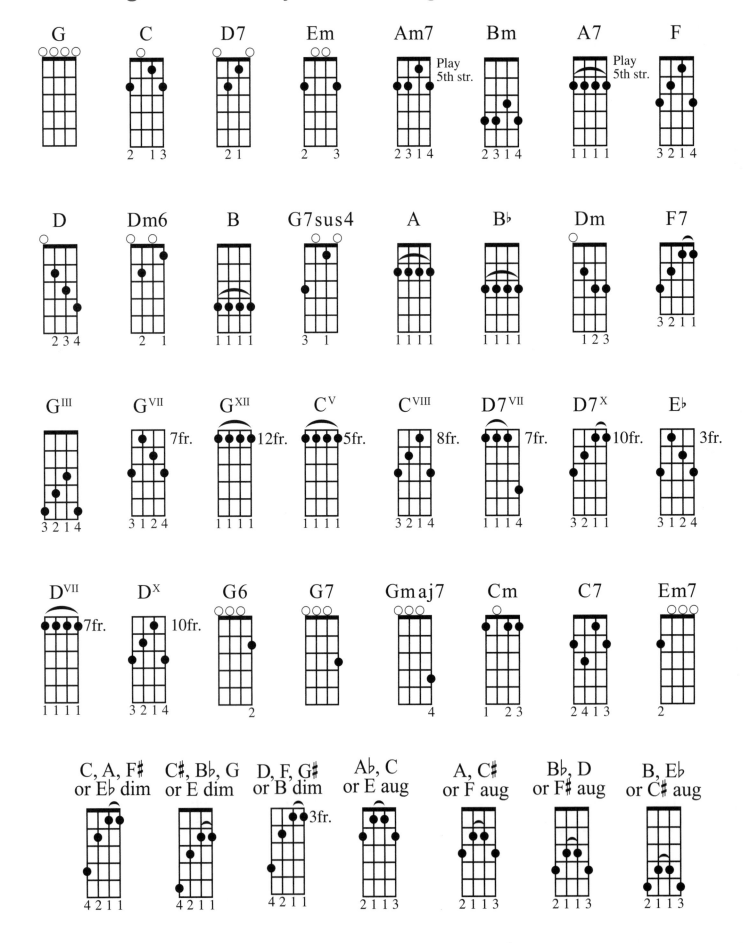

Chord Diagrams for Banjo in C Tuning: G C G B D

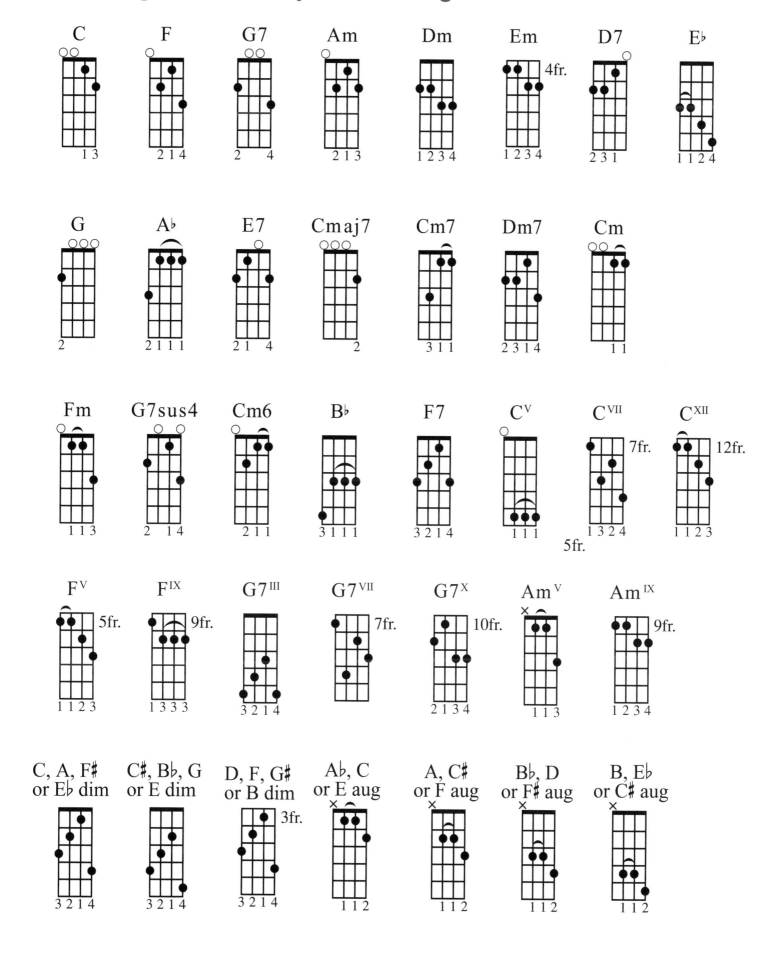

Getting Acquainted with Music

Although this book does not use traditional music notation, we are including these pages in case you use other published material for reference.

Musical sounds are indicated by symbols called *notes.* Their time value is determined by their color (white or black) and by stems or flags attached to the note.

The Staff

The notes are named after the first seven letters of the alphabet (A–G), endlessly repeated to embrace the entire range of musical sound. The name and pitch of the note is determined by its position on five horizontal lines and the spaces between, called the *staff.*

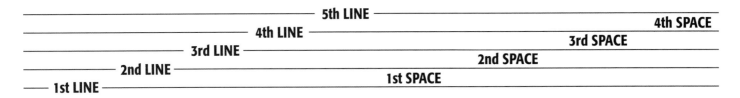

Measures

Music is divided into equal parts called *measures.* One measure is divided from another by a *bar line.*

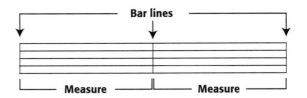

Clefs

During the evolution of music notation, the staff had from 2 to 20 lines, and symbols were invented to locate certain lines and the pitch of the note on that line. These symbols are called *clefs.*

Music for banjo is written in the *G clef* or *treble clef.* Originally, the Gothic letter G was used on a four-line staff to establish the pitch of G.

   This grew into the modern notation:

Naming the Notes

Notes are referred to by letters. The only letters used are: A B C D
E F and G. Here are all the notes playable on the first five frets in
the G tuning:

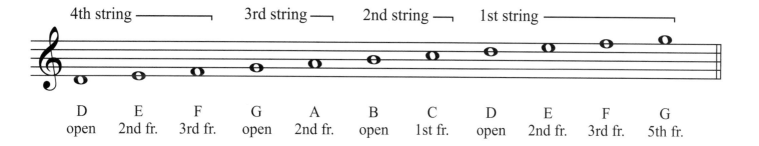

In C tuning, all the notes on the top strings are the same. The
notes on the 4th string are:

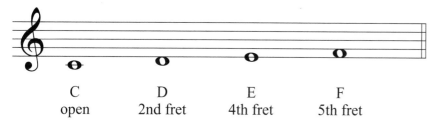

Rhythm

Rhythm is organized by rest and note values. Both are indicated
by their shape and appearance. The diagrams below break
down the relationship between rest values and note values,
respectively.

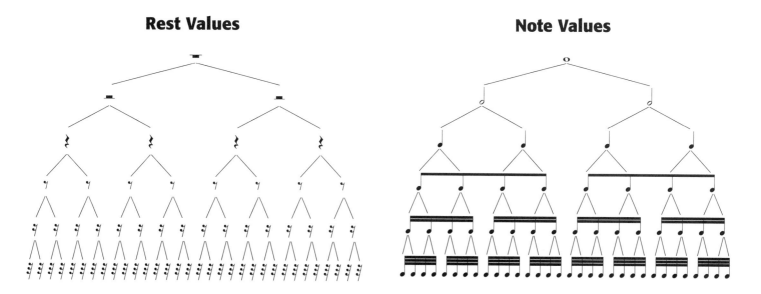

Flats ♭, Sharps ♯, and Naturals ♮

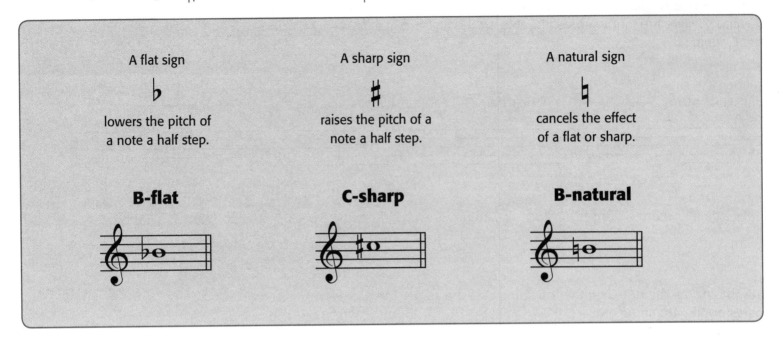

Key Signatures

To make the writing process easier, we can indicate the flats or sharps to be used in a composition at the beginning of the piece. This is called a *key signature* and tells the performer that the *accidentals* (flats and sharps) indicated are in effect throughout the piece.

For example, the F♯ in this key signature, which appears on the top line of the staff immediately following the clef, indicates that all of the F's in this composition are to be played F♯.

Additional Information on Banjo Heads, Strings, Bridges, and Fingerpicks

Banjo tone is partly a function of the tightness of the head. The tighter the head, the crisper the sound. Most bluegrass players keep the head really tight. The tautness is adjustable by using a tool that looks like a skate key. If you tighten the head, turn the key only a quarter turn for each bracket. If your head is really loose, you may need to tighten all of the brackets three or even four times.

You also should keep the tuning gears tight so that they don't slip. If the tuning gears slip, it is impossible to keep the banjo in tune. You will need to buy a very small screwdriver and occasionally tighten the gears.

Choice of Banjo Heads

There are three types of banjo heads that are currently available. The calfskin head is not used in bluegrass, so we won't discuss it in detail here. The majority of bluegrass players use a plastic head, but there is also a fiberskyn head that is a sort of compromise between calfskin and the plastic head. If you plan to play the banjo in a variety of styles, you may find that the fibreskyn head is the most suitable for your needs.

If you tighten the head too much it will crack, and you will need to replace it. This is a rare occurrence, but some bluegrass players tighten the head so much that this becomes a real possibility.

Strings, Bridges, and Fingerpicks

Many bluegrass players prefer light-gauge strings, but some use medium, or medium-light strings. Light strings sound brighter and are easier to finger with the left hand. Medium-gauge strings provide a stronger bass sound. Heavy-gauge strings are also available, but very few people use them. Sometimes when you change from a medium gauge to a light-gauge string, the banjo will make a buzzing sound. People who play classical music on the banjo use nylon strings.

Most contemporary players use a bridge that has three "feet" that hold it on the banjo head. Recently more bridges have become available that offer additional features and are more expensive. But before you spend $25 on a bridge, you might want to hear the same banjo played with that bridge and a more traditional one. If you feel there is little difference, why invest the extra money?

Fingerpicks come in different gauges of thickness and are made of various materials. You should be concerned with the fit of the picks on your fingers, and about the sound that the picks get. Not many players use plastic fingerpicks on the banjo, although quite a few guitarists prefer them. Many banjo players use plastic thumb picks, and some prefer the steel picks. Some players are not able to use steel thumb picks, because they find themselves unable to avoid a good deal of pick noise. There are a bewildering number of fingerpicks available these days and many of them are quite expensive.

Keep your banjo away from radiators. Although shipping banjos on an airplane is somewhat less dangerous than it is for guitars, the banjo headstock could be damaged in the luggage compartment of an airplane. Consequently, make every effort to carry your banjo on the plane. Hard cases and padded gig bags are now readily available for banjos. Remember that when you ship a banjo or even take it out of an airplane luggage rack or a car trunk, the bridge of the instrument often moves. The placement of the bridge should be re-calculated when you get to your destination.

Final Thoughts

Listen to as many other banjo players as you can. If you are patient, you will be surprised at how rapidly you will be able to sound good and have fun with the instrument. Best of luck!

CERTIFICATE OF PROMOTION

ALFRED'S BASIC BANJO METHOD

This certifies that

_____

has mastered
Alfred's Basic Banjo Method 1
and is promoted to
Alfred's Basic Banjo Method 2

Teacher _____

Date _____